TAKE DOMINION

DOMINION IS YOURS FOR THE TAKING

IFY
IKEKHUA

TAKE DOMINION

First Edition: November 2018

ISBN: 978-0578415215

Printed in the United States of America

Cover Design by Enoch Odu
Edited by Amy Noelck

*This book is dedicated to anyone who has experienced
the loss of a loved one, the demise of a marriage,
an injustice or abuse of any kind.
It's time to Take Dominion.*

CONTENTS

FOREWORD

When I first met Ify in 2017, I was impressed by her love of God, her humility, and her innate sense of right and wrong. She knew she had been treated wrongly by her ex-husband, but she was determined to not be defined by what she had suffered—and she had suffered much. I detected in her a strength of character, purpose, and a lack of self-centeredness. I was aware of how much strength she would need to overcome the lack of joy that threatened her.

She needed a little help at that time, and I wanted to not only help her out of her current need but to also become her friend. I'm proud to now call her a friend.

Ify's authenticity, intelligence, and determination are hallmarks of her personality. She trusts God to guide her, and He has brought her to this point in her life. She has overcome the obstacles to her well-being by trusting Him to imbue her life with the fruit of the Holy Spirit: love, joy, peace, patience, kindness, goodness, faithfulness, gentleness, and self-control.

In 2018, Ify came to visit, and it was wonderful to see her looking radiant! She had met and married a wonderful Christian man, her life was stable, her children and her mom were all doing well, and all love her husband. And, praise God, they are expecting! Yet, with all Ify has been through—she only wanted to find out how she could contribute to the ministry that my husband and I founded.

This book is a testament to this strong young woman's dedication to God and His Holy Word.

Judith Vaughan
Founder and CEO of John 3:16 Transitional Family Housing

INTRODUCTION: TAKE DOMINION

I know what it is to have a broken heart and an aching soul from the hurt of life's experiences. I know what it's like to have placed my hope in a dream, only to have it shatter before my very eyes. I know what it's like to want to give up and throw in the towel when everything in life appears to be barren and hopeless.

But I also know what it's like to overcome.

I know that we can recover from any loss. I know that our hearts can be mended from any form of heartache. I know that we can rebuild our broken dreams. I know that we can speak life into dead things and watch them breathe again before our very eyes.

I know, because I have.

Over the years, I have watched my life evolve from a place of brokenness to a place of wholeness. I'm continuing to take back the power that God placed inside of me from the foundations of the world. I'm assuming the position of dominion every day of my life—a position that God designed for every one of us from the beginning of time. We may experience trouble in this life, but we are not distressed. We may be perplexed, but we are not in despair. We may be persecuted, but we are not forsaken. We may be cast down, but we are not destroyed (2 Corinthians 4:8).

We survive and overcome because we are created to dominate kingdoms, territories, and every impossible situation in our lives. That is why you are still standing. That is why the troubles you've faced haven't taken you out. God has been preserving you so that you can discover what He has placed inside of you. You have, within you, the power to rise above any situation that seems insurmountable.

This book is designed to help you take your rightful place on earth. You were created to have dominion. You are the head and not the tail. You are above every circumstance in your life. You are higher than any situation confronting you right now. Dominion is yours for the taking. Genesis 1:26 (NKJV) says, "Then God said, let Us make man in Our image, according to Our likeness; let them have dominion over the fish of the sea, over the birds of the air, and over the cattle, over all the earth and over every creeping thing that creeps on the earth."

Our responsibility is to take what God has already allowed us to have: Dominion is ours for the taking.

It's one thing to be given dominion but it's another to take hold of what has been given. That's the part I had to discover for myself. To have dominion, we must recognize our domain. And our domain is the earth God created for us.

Dominion represents authority—it's the power to rule. But power is not passive, and neither is authority. You rule with power and you take authority over your domain. That's how you dominate!

As you read this book, I pray you would recognize and begin to activate the power you already have within you to dominate any situation in your life. This book is instructional, prophetic, and very timely for anyone who seeks to take dominion over any area of their lives. It is designed to stir you up to make the tough decisions required for success and to take the necessary action steps for dominion in the area you were created to function in.

Dominion is a mentality and it is yours for the taking!

1
WE ALL CRAVE SUCCESS

As soon as I learned to read and write at the young age of three, I had the desire to succeed at everything I did. While this may seem like a special trait to possess at that age, it wasn't. Everything that God has created is made to succeed. Everyone hungers and thirsts for success because it is in our nature to succeed.

My desire for wanting to succeed in life only grew stronger as I grew older. There was something in me that demanded excellence in all I did. I couldn't stand the thought of settling for anything less than what I knew I could accomplish.

I was often misunderstood by my peers for wanting more than what seemed normal for a young girl, but their perception didn't deter me from reaching higher. The more people tried to limit my ability to succeed, the more determined I became to defy the limitations they tried to place on me.

I knew God was calling me to become all that He created me to be, so I couldn't let anyone's contrary opinion stop me. I knew I would be successful. I knew this when I was only three years old. Success is like a buzzword. Everyone is attracted to it. We all get inspired by it and if we are honest, we will admit that we do aspire to be successful in some way. However, there's a misconception of what success really is. There seems to be a standard for success that is being promoted all around us and if you don't meet this so-called "standard," then you are not successful.

In the western world, we have painted a picture of what success ought to look like. If you make a six-figure income, live in a luxury home, drive a fancy car, and can afford to travel to exotic places around the world then you are considered "successful." Success has become all about one's possessions and the recognition that follows suit.

We live in a very confusing time where success is measured by the number of followers one has on social media. Countless people appear to be successful on social media while struggling every day to keep up with the public image they have created for themselves. There seems to be a disparity between a person's real life and their stage-managed life.

Some people are trying so hard to measure up to other people's success simply because they want to be considered successful themselves. We all want to have a public image that exudes success. As such, some people feel obligated to out-do someone else just so that they can feel successful themselves.

Society has sold us the "Keeping up with the Joneses" idea that we've got to be better than our neighbor in order to be considered successful, and many have bought into this fallacy. This misconstrued idea of success has led to intense competition amongst individuals, businesses, companies, and brands as they have become solely preoccupied with out-doing each other. Inevitably, they miss the opportunity to become the best versions of themselves.

In an attempt to pursue this false idea of success, many have found themselves in marriages they shouldn't have entered, careers they shouldn't have pursued, contracts they shouldn't have signed, houses they shouldn't have purchased, and paths they shouldn't have traveled. I am up for being motivated by successful people; however, I don't subscribe to their success being your benchmark. **A person's success ought to inspire you to be your best self, not to engineer you to be like them.**

Another person's success isn't designed to make you cynical, hateful, or jealous. On the contrary, you ought to celebrate other's success regardless of where you are on your own journey. If you keep a positive mental attitude and continue working on yourself, you too will gain success in life.

Success is a mentality. The world-renowned martial artist, Bruce Lee, so truthfully stated, "As you think, so shall you become." The central purpose of having someone to look up to is for your belief in yourself to be heightened to the point where you can take massive action and reach your highest potential.

Success is discovering and fulfilling the purpose for which you were created. Your success has nothing to do with anyone but you. Your neighbor's success is only an indication that yours is possible. You were created to succeed, and you don't have to be anyone but you to achieve success.

In all humility and reverence to God, you can do anything and everything you set your mind to do. Napoleon Hill said, "Whatever your mind can conceive and believe, it can achieve." The power to create the life of your dreams lies within you. You already possess everything you could ever need to have an incredible life. Your solution does not lie outside of yourself.

Whatever you desire to have that you have not yet acquired, you simply haven't created. Whatever you desire to have, you must create for yourself. If what you want doesn't exist, then it's your obligation to create it.

God created the whole world and all that is in it. Most importantly, He created you. Therefore, you were created by a creator. You were created by God to be creative. You are a creator just like your Father. You were created to do what your Father does. You were created to create solutions, ideas, opportunities, wealth—and anything and everything else that you can imagine with your creative mind.

Those who believe they were created to be creative are the ones making things happen. Others often refer to these types of people as being successful, and rightly so. However, they are not an elite group of people. Everyone was created to succeed in life simply because God created us all.

The reality is, not everyone believes they were created to succeed. Some do, and some don't. Those who do are the ones winning in life and those who don't have yet to experience the fruit a winning life can offer. But no matter what your current situation is, you already possess everything it takes to make it better.

Paul acknowledged this truth in Philippians 4:13 (NKJV) when he said, "I can do all things through Christ who strengthens me."

You can do anything. Not by your power, but by the creative power of God at work within you. Therefore, if it's a thing, you can do it. If it's a dream, you can accomplish it. If it's a problem, you can solve it. If it's a test, you can pass it. If it's a mountain, you can move it. If it's a dragon, you can slay it. If it's an empire, you can build it.

You are powerful! You are so much more than what other people think or say you are (or even what you think and say about yourself). You are a child of God, and therefore, you ought to think like God, speak like God, act like God, and live like God because you were made in the image and likeness of God.

When people look at you, they ought to see God in you because you are His child. Parents will often tell you that their children not only look like them physically, but that they have taken on their mannerisms, postures, attitudes, specific displays of creativity, and so on.

If this is true about parents and their biological children, then you ought to believe that you also display certain characteristics and attributes of your Father in heaven. You are not only a resemblance of your biological parents, but you are also a spitting image of God Himself. Before the foundations of the world, God knew He was going to fashion you just like Himself. This is the whole essence of who you are; and until you understand whose you are, nothing else will matter. You were predestined to be great and mighty because your Father is great and mighty. You were designed for excellence because your Father is excellent. This truth ought to be ingrained in you if you are going to live a life of distinction.

When I discovered this truth for myself, I began to redefine myself. I began to speak about myself differently.

I began to reprogram my mind to believe what God says about me: He says, I am fearfully and wonderfully made (Psalms 139:14). He says I am the apple of His eye (Psalms 17:8, Zechariah 2:18). He says I am the child of the Most High (Psalms 82:6). And, He is saying the same about you.

What God says about you supersedes what anyone else says about you. We simply have to learn to agree with it. Other people's opinions about you are irrelevant so long as they aren't in alignment with God's word over your life.

Don't accept everything someone else says to you as truth without first comparing it to God's Word. Don't accept any falsehood that is being said about you; rather, attack every lie spoken against you with the truth of God's Word. You've got to attack whatever is challenging the truth of God's Word over your life. Yes! Attack whatever is attacking you.

Attack unbelief with faith. Attack ignorance with wisdom. Attack fear with courage. Attack negativity with positivity. Attack evil with good. Attack sadness with joy. Attack poverty with generosity. Attack sickness with wellness. Attack laziness with vitality. This is how you take dominion!

You don't have to condone the things you don't want. If you don't like the way things are going in your life, you owe it to yourself to do something about it. You are responsible for the outcome of your life. It's about time you take ownership of your life and stop looking for reasons to justify where you are. **You can either spend your time creating the life you know you deserve, or you can spend your time refining your excuses to justify what you have failed to create.** You alone are responsible for success in your life. You were created by

God with a spirit, a creative ability, a physique, a personality, and the unique talents to live life like no other.

Your greatness was placed inside of you by God. He hid the most valuable treasure right inside of you: Inside of you lies a creator. Inside of you lies a transformer. Inside of you lies the solution that the world is looking for. You are so much more than you are manifesting right now. There is another dimension to your greatness. There are no limits to what you can do. Just because you haven't done something doesn't mean you are incapable of doing it. You are capable of doing whatever you believe you can.

BORN TO WIN

I was born and raised in Nigeria and I am very proud of my cultural heritage. It is important to acknowledge that no one chooses the place of their birth or the family they are born into. We don't get to pick our skin color and other physical attributes that we possess. Each one of us came into this world by divine arrangement.

Your cultural background is not a disadvantage, but an advantage that guarantees your authenticity. Rather than wish you were born into a different family or a different part of the world, choose to embrace your identity and fall in love with who you are. We've got to learn to love ourselves—flaws and all. We've got to get comfortable with ourselves because when it's all said and done, no one will spend more time with you than you.

No one will ever put more value on you than the value you have chosen to put on yourself. Your worth is not determined by appearance or any other attribute you possess or don't possess. Your value lies in the understanding of who you are. You are of God. You are inestimable. You are incomparable. Although you didn't choose your family or the place of your birth, you can choose to live the life you were created to live: A life of dominion.

How you got here is not as important as discovering why you are here. When God made man, He gave him dominion over all that He created. Dominion is your birthright. Man was not born to compete, rather he was born to dominate. Anyone who strives to compete with others lacks this understanding.

Genesis 1:26 (ESV) says, "Then God said let us make man in our image, in our likeness, so that they may rule over the fish of the sea and over the fowl of the air and over every creeping thing that creeps upon the earth."

Notice the verse does not say that man was given dominion over his fellow man. Therefore, you were not given dominion over other people—you were given dominion over the resources on earth. Your dominion is not a product of your location or nationality. It is a product of a divine setup established by God at the beginning of creation.

As a teenager, whenever I saw the people I admired on television or in person, I wished I was part of their family or at least part of their circle of friends. I thought if only I was like them or related to them, then I would have an incredible life. As I grew older, I got tired of wishing for the life I desired to have. I began to realize that it is my obligation to create the life I desire to have. Too often, we spend so much time wishing and hoping for the life we desire instead of creating it. The reason being, it's much easier to wish for something than it is to create it. Wishing takes little or no mental effort, whereas creativity demands much more than just wishful thinking. Anyone can wish for anything but not everyone can make that wish a reality.

If you are going to live a life of dominion, then you must create for yourself what you desire to have. The people who create solutions are those who dominate their industry. Ironically, those who fail to create solutions only wish to dominate. The key to dominion is creativity. It's very plain and simple: become creative and you will dominate. Dominators are creators.

YOUR GIFTS UNLOCK DOORS

There are a few experiences I had in my late twenties that prompted me to begin writing this book. It all began in 2009 when I arrived in the United States. Prior to my arrival, my life was anything but ordinary for a young girl from Nigeria.

I was the youngest child in my family and obtained my first college degree at the age of 20. At that time, I had no doubt in my mind that I was going to impact my world. I was young, full of life, and ready to do big things. I had tried a couple of career opportunities and I hit a home run when I became a radio personality without any experience in broadcasting or public speaking.

Proverbs 18:16 (NKJV) says, "A man's gift makes room for him, and brings him before great men."

It was evident that my gifts had landed me a job that I was not technically qualified for. When you are gifted in an area, you don't struggle to perform. But make no mistake, your gift can never be a substitute for hard work. Just because you are gifted doesn't mean you are exempt from work. You've got to be diligent! Your gifts will announce you, but your diligence will keep you relevant and effective.

Working at the radio station gave me an opportunity to develop my gifts in communication. It is where I learned that I had a voice created to be heard. In that season, I knew I was going to use my voice to liberate people all over the world, but I had no idea how. My family believed in me so much that my sister told me I was going to become the Oprah Winfrey of my generation. That statement of belief got me excited and I began to see myself through a different lens. But as time went by, I realized that attempting to measure up to someone else's blessings causes a lot of negative pressure. God is the only one who can bless a man. God didn't promise to do for you what He did for someone else. He promises to be with you just like He has been with those who have gone ahead of you.

As I write this book, I have no desire to become the next Oprah Winfrey. Though I have incredible respect and adoration for who Oprah is, I've come to realize that I cannot be like Oprah Winfrey or anyone else, even if I tried. But what I do know, is that the same God who was and is with Oprah Winfrey is the same God who is with me. The same God who has granted her success beyond comprehension is the same God who is granting me permission to succeed. And it is far better to be an authentic version of yourself than an imitation of someone else.

When you are authentic, you are unstoppable. When you refuse to be anyone else but you, you place yourself in a class of your own. You are in a place where your best self has no choice but to emerge. Each of us was made for something unique; however, we can only perform uniquely when we are in our own lane. That which only you can do can only be done when you are authentic and true to yourself. Your authenticity stirs up your ingenuity. If you are going to perform at your peak, then you must be authentic.

Now, it is possible to be authentic and still not see the fullness of your potential. The people you choose to surround yourself with are very critical to your success, as they determine in part the scope of what you can discover about yourself. I couldn't see myself becoming a world renown speaker, but my sister could. I knew I had a voice, but I had not yet learned how to use it effectively. I was excited to hear my sister speak so highly of me, but I knew I had to do something extraordinary to make my dream a reality.

Thomas Jefferson once said, "If you want something you've never had, you've got to do something you've never done." Over time, it became clear to me that it is my responsibility to raise my standards and demand more of myself every day. I realized successful people don't stumble upon success; on the contrary, they are very intentional about the way they live their lives. They make things happen through their beliefs, actions, persistence, discipline, and a strong desire to see their dreams become reality. Just because you have great dreams doesn't mean you are going to accomplish them without a fight.

I had a wonderful childhood experience and I don't remember not having the things I needed growing up. I never experienced anything traumatic until I became an adult. In 2004, my sister was involved in a horrible accident that almost claimed her life, shortly followed by the death of my father in 2007. For the first time in my life, I felt robbed. My father and I were great friends. He had a special kind of love for me. He entrusted me with a lot of responsibilities around the house because he knew I had what it took to manage a home. He saw the leader in me, even when I had no clue what leadership was about. I had a great sense of responsibility early on in life because of the way my father raised me. I never relied on others for what I knew I could provide for myself. I took charge whenever the occasion called for it. I was fierce and fearless.

By 2008, I got married and relocated to the United States the following year. Shortly after, in 2013, I was divorced and became a single parent of two beautiful children. A year after that, I lost one of my brothers. By this point, I literally felt as though my life was spinning out of control. These traumatic events happened so fast, within such a short space of time, that it gave me little to no time to process them. There was no time to pause and grieve the losses I had encountered. I was broken, hurt, and angry. Coming to America seemed to have torn my life apart, and I was left alone to face the darkest season of my life.

Little did I know that the darkest season of my life would birth the brightest season of my life. How ironic! How can the worst of times become the best of times? How can your victory be hidden in your tribulation? The best answer I can come up with is: God made it so. This is God's setup! God designed life in a way where our greatest defeats become our greatest victories.

2 Corinthians 5:15 (NIV) says, "And he died for all, that those who live should no longer live for themselves but for him who died for them and was raised again."

The Son of God, Jesus Christ, had to die so you and I could have life. In other words, we have life because Christ died. Without His death and resurrection, there would be no life. 2 Corinthians 8:9 (ESV) adds to this theory saying, "For you know the grace of our Lord Jesus Christ, that though he was rich, yet for your sake he became poor, so that you by his poverty might become rich."

So, it's not surprising that your problem carries your solution with it. Your ministry lies in your misery. The cure you are looking for lies in the sickness you are suffering from. I would even go so far as to say that anyone who has never failed at anything has likely never tasted success because failure births success. What a brilliant design by God Himself!

James 1:2-3 (NIV) says, "Consider it pure joy, my brothers and sisters, whenever you face trials of many kinds, because you know that the testing of your faith produces perseverance."

When you are praying for elevation, you are also saying, "God, I am ready to endure tribulations." You are signing up to be challenged because that is the only way you can grow. You are aligning yourself with God's design for life. You are willing to pass through the burning furnace because you now know that you will come out on the other side, shining bright.

Being a single parent with two children made my life tougher than it would have been otherwise. I began to see how one major decision had affected the quality of my life. I had entered into a marriage that was founded on deception with no vision for the future. The foundation of a thing always determines the outcome and if the foundation is faulty, the whole structure will eventually crumble.

For the first time in my life, I experienced unimaginable physical, mental, and emotional abuse at the hands of my ex-husband. I was assaulted, beat down, and kicked to the streets; stripped of everything but my dignity and my faith in God. I had to start life all over again with nothing but the breath I carried in my lungs. My condition was so bad that I didn't see the purpose of living any longer. But I was reminded in my darkest moments that God had not brought me to a foreign country to abandon me. God promised never to leave or forsake me (Deuteronomy 31:6). I believed His Word then and I still believe it now.

Nobody told me the road would be easy, but I refused to believe that God had brought me this far to leave me by the wayside. During my divorce, I battled with child custody, child support, and joint conservatorship—all of which were strange to me, but I learned fast. The more issues I had to deal with, the more determined I was to live the life I was born to live: a life of dominion. I refused to settle for a status that read: broke, divorced, single parent in dire need of help. Rather, I was bent on pursuing my dream of becoming a transformational speaker and best-selling author at all costs.

We often say we will pursue our dreams at all costs, but when we are eventually faced with the cost of our dreams, we tend to reevaluate our desire. The truth is, your dreams will cost you everything. You've got to be willing to give up who you are to become who you were created to be. In other words, you must be born again. You must die to who you are in order to be re-born into who you can become.

As a little girl, I remember standing in front of the mirror and speaking into an imaginary microphone (my hairbrush) as though I had an audience listening to me. I did this quite often and it made me very happy. When anyone asked me who I was, I would respond confidently, "I am an English girl." I spoke and acted like royalty. My mother was fascinated by my way of life at that tender age and she recounts the experience to date. As children, when we went to birthday parties and it was time for the celebrant to cut their cake, if they cried and refused to cut their cake, I would lean over and help them do it. I was unafraid to lead, even as a child, and I knew exactly what I wanted out of life.

However, being certain of my identity didn't stop life from happening to me. Being born again doesn't exempt you from life's challenges, it only provides an anchor for your soul amid the challenges of life.

Although my life didn't turn out the way I had planned, I wouldn't trade who I have become for anything in the world. Looking back now, I see why I had to go through what I went through. No one wants to revisit the past, but the past is the very thing that has shaped the life we have today.

It is a healthy practice to view your life in retrospect from time to time. It gives you an opportunity to get comfortable with what has happened in your life. The past will always reveal the patterns in your life. If you pay close attention to your past, you will see patterns of success and failure. But no matter how you feel about your past, you cannot change it so why live in guilt when you can embrace it and be free? You cannot undo your past; however, you can change the way you feel about it.

When I look back at my life, I can see how far God has brought me. My past reassures me of the unconditional love My Father has for me. Sometimes we avoid the past completely, not realizing that failing to learn from past mistakes will result in repeated mistakes. I grew up hearing the phrase, "Experience is the best teacher." I didn't quite understand the meaning of this phrase until I began to consciously recount my own experiences. Then I realized that if I continue to do the same things that caused me pain, I will end up receiving nothing but more pain. The same approach will lead to the same outcome, but a different approach will lead to a different outcome.

It's time to examine your life. Take inventory of the patterns you see. If your outcomes are favorable, then reinforce your approach. But if your outcomes are unfavorable, then it's time for a change. You can learn about life one of two ways: through your own experiences or through the experiences of others. You can save yourself years of pain if you choose to review your past and those of other people. We can avoid the recurrence of unpleasant experiences if we cultivate the habit of learning from these two sources. So often, we think the past lies only in what happened 10 or 20 years ago, but every passing moment belongs to the past. The last hour, what happened yesterday, last week, last year—they all belong in the past.

TAKE DOMINION

2
QUIT THE BLAME GAME

When I arrived in the United States, I was excited to meet my ex-husband and his family. We were newly married, and I thought we were going to live happily ever after. In less than two weeks after my arrival, I discovered the shocking lifestyle of the person I had married. The person I thought I had married was completely different from the person I was living with. The man I was living with and married to was addicted to pornography. I was alarmed to discover the extent to which he was hooked on this way of living and I thought it was my responsibility to fix him. This only triggered his resentment of me and consequently, physical abuse toward me.

Now, I must say that prior to marrying this man, I saw several signs that indicated the relationship was toxic. However, I paid no attention to these red flags until they became life-threatening. Problems don't go away simply because we ignore them. When we ignore problems, they only get bigger and more dangerous. I was responsible for the ugly experience I had in the hands of my ex-husband. It's easier to play the role of a victim in life when things don't turn out the way we planned, but the true test of maturity is when we take responsibility for the events that happen in our lives. When we blame others for things that go wrong in our lives, we give them the power to control us.

Assuming the role of a victim renders you powerless

and makes the other party very powerful. Flip the script, change your approach, and assume the role of a victor. I am responsible for the outcome of my life and so are you. I cannot blame my ex-husband for treating me the way he did. After all, I made the decision to marry him even when I saw danger written all over him in bold letters. You are where you are today because of the decisions you made yesterday, and you've got to acknowledge that in order to change tomorrow.

Some decisions are more critical than others. The decision to marry someone is far more critical than the decision to buy a car. The decision to marry someone can alter the rest of your life, so it should not be made casually or ignorantly. I didn't enter my previous marriage casually, but I did enter it ignorantly. In my case, I was unaware of how damaging a toxic relationship could be until I began to experience it for myself.

It's interesting how much time couples spend picking out the perfect wedding dress or venue but fail to study what makes a healthy marriage possible. It's your responsibility to study marriage as instituted by God before walking down the aisle and saying, "I do." Everyone wants a successful marriage, but few take the time to study relationships and the components that make it work. Most couples don't seek help early enough and wait until their marriage is on the brink of divorce before they find themselves in a counselor's office trying to repair what is already broken. Sadly, most marriages that start this way often end in divorce.

After the birth of my first son, I resolved that our children were not going to witness any form of domestic abuse in our home. Most of the unresolved issues we face in our adult life stem from the experiences we had as children. I found out that my ex-husband had grown up seeing his father physically abusing his mother. His mother disclosed this information to me when I was being physically abused by her son. Children will grow up to do whatever is modeled in front of them. Children will not do what you say, they will do what they see you do.

My ex-husband witnessed domestic abuse in his family while growing up, so he was desensitized to abuse of any kind. While abuse was a horrific experience for me, it was a way of life for him. The only tools he knew to use to resolve conflicts were wicked and violent. At the time, I couldn't understand why he behaved the way he did, and I took it upon myself to try to change him.

Most women remain in abusive relationships, failing to realize that their decision to stay destroys not only their lives but the lives of their children and the other family members involved. When my son was about 9 months old, there was another episode of domestic abuse in our home, and for the first time in over a year of an abusive cycle, I made a 911 call. Soon thereafter, my abuser was arrested. But upon his return home from jail, things grew from bad to worse.

At this point, it was clear I had made a mistake that was ravaging my life. Living with my ex-husband was hell on earth. Finally, one night I determined enough was enough. I packed up my personal belongings, left with my child, and never looked back.

YOUR IDENTITY IS HIS IDENTITY

The only reason I was able to leave the abuse from my ex-husband was that I was reminded of who I am: A child of God.

I knew I was precious in the sight of my Father. I knew I was royalty. I knew I deserved to be treated with love and respect. I knew I had the spirit of God in me. The knowledge I had about myself made me unapologetic about my decision to seek a better way of living.

If you don't know who you are, people will tell you who you are not. Your answer to the question, "Who are you?" will determine how you live your life. How would you live your life if you were the son or daughter of a king? Differently, right? Well, begin to live that way, because your Father owns the universe. Your Father is the King of kings and the Lord of lords.

When we talk about identity, we immediately think of the country or race a person is from. A person could be identified by their culture, language, physical appearance, or amongst other things—but that's not all there is to that person. It's important to know your cultural roots because they define you in part, but knowing your spiritual roots is the greatest discovery of all time. Your spiritual root is the very essence of who you are.

Zechariah 12:1 (NKJV) says, "Thus says the Lord, who stretches out the heavens, lays the foundation of the earth, and forms the spirit of man within him." Man is a spirit and God chose you and me before we were even born into this world. Before you were born into your earthly family, you were already part of God's family. You are God's masterpiece and

He created you for good works. That's who you are!

Every living thing gives birth to its kind. A lion gives birth to a lion, an eagle gives birth to an eagle, and likewise, a God gives birth to a god. If we are born of God, then we are gods. Your identity is in your creator. You are the child of a King and His name is Jesus Christ. You are a prince or princess because your father is King of all. By Him, you reign and decree justice. Just like your Father, you have creative powers and you can speak things into existence. We were born into this world on purpose because God's word says, "Before I formed you in the womb I knew you, before you were born I set you apart; I appointed you as a prophet to the nations" (Jeremiah 1:5 NIV).

This truth ought to be ingrained in your mind, soul, and spirit. You are an original. You were thought of before you were created. God put in you everything you need to be free, happy, successful, and victorious. You don't have to struggle with your identity. God doesn't relate to us according to our nationality, gender, or skin color—rather, He relates to us as spiritual beings.

Today, I am honored to be a citizen of two great countries, but that is not where my true identity lies. I was raised in a Christian home, but until I had a personal encounter with Jesus, my identity was unknown to me. I couldn't quite understand why I had a great passion to live a life of contribution until I realized my purpose.

You and I were born with a purpose. Sometimes we make the mistake of comparing ourselves to others and we often discredit ourselves by thinking we don't have what it takes to live an extraordinary life. The truth is, we do have all it takes to become all that God intended for us to become. Until you understand who you are, you will be labeled for what you are not, and life will seem worthless.

Understanding who we are comes from spending time with our Father through prayer, meditation, and the study of His Word. If we fail to practice walking with God every day, life will compel us to seek Him in tears. Troubles seem to draw us closer to God, and God wants us to call out to Him in times of trouble, but we ought to seek Him even when there is peace. We've got to be hungry and thirsty for God Himself— not only for what He can do for us.

Troubles will humble us and make us fall on our knees in total surrender. We can reach heaven when our knees are on the ground. The greatest battles in life are not the ones fought with weapons but the ones we fight on our knees. God wants us to acknowledge Him in all we do. Going down on your knees is not only a sign of humility but an indication that we recognize the presence of a higher authority over our lives. That is why the Bible says that at the mention of the name of Jesus every knee must bow and every tongue must confess that He is Lord (Philippians 2: 10-11).

Your belief and declaration that Jesus Christ is Lord is the acceptance of your position as a son or daughter of God. Who you are in Christ is who you are in life. Your identity is not found in your condition, because your condition is subject to change. On the contrary, your identity is found in your position as a child of God and that will never change. You cannot cease to become a child of God. Nothing can separate you from the everlasting love of your Father. Don't believe anything else about your identity. Believe and declare that you are the child of the Most High God.

When an abusive relationship tried to define me, the Spirit of God in me revolted against it. When you are saturated with the knowledge of who you are in Christ, it becomes impossible for anyone to tell you otherwise. My ex-husband tried to convince me that I wouldn't survive without him. He threatened me so that I would put up with his acts of wickedness, but his words only stirred up the lioness within me.

The Bible tells me that God is the Lion of the Tribe of Judah (Revelation 5:5), and I am born of God; therefore, I am a lioness. The Spirit of God in me was constantly at war with the spirit of the enemy. The battle you are in is not against flesh and blood. You are in a fight against principalities and powers of darkness. When people wage war against you, they are waging war against God—and God cannot be defeated. No decree spoken by any man or woman can come to pass in your life unless God commands it.

CHASE AFTER DESTINY

Once you have understood your identity, the next thing you need to discover is your purpose. Your purpose is simply what you are living for. Your purpose is what drives you and makes you do what you do. Don't get your job confused with your purpose. Your job is what you do, while your purpose is the reason behind what you do.

You are here for a purpose—not just to go to school, get a

job, get married, have children, get old, and eventually retire. All of these plans are good, but your life's purpose is much bigger than all of these things put together. There's a greater call upon your life. The world is waiting for the manifestation of the children of God, and that includes you and me.

Do you ever wonder what drives you to want to have a family, a job, a business, or a good life? That's your purpose! My purpose is to help people birth their dreams, despite what they have been through. My purpose is to help women who are hurting from the pain of domestic abuse, divorce, or separation so they can become all that God has created them to be. I want to see people set free from the hurt of past relationships. I want to see the wounded healed. I want to see the broken put back together again. I want to see the hopeless restored. I want to utilize all of God's deposit in me to bring about change around me. God has given me a unique path, so I can help others experience freedom from the shackles that have held them bound.

Once I was broken beyond words, but God, through His infinite mercy made me whole again. Being whole doesn't mean you will never be broken, but you serve a God who specializes in fixing broken people. The good news I bring to you is this: God's grace is available to everyone and anyone who would reach out to receive it.

It's possible to be whole again. It doesn't matter the extent of your brokenness, God can still put you back together. No one has the final say over your life, except God. It's not over until God says so. No can put a period where God has placed a comma. You don't need anyone else's validation to feel complete. You are enough. You have all it takes to live the life of your dreams.

When I was pregnant with my second child, I came down with Chickenpox in my third trimester. Two days prior, I received a call from a sheriff informing me that I had divorce papers from my husband. In the same month, I had an immigration interview that was to determine my stay in the United States. While I was lying on the hospital bed on admission for Chickenpox, I had several thoughts come to my mind: I thought of giving up and forsaking all I had labored for. It seemed easier for me to give up when I was faced with the scars from the Chickenpox, the shame of going through a divorce, the pain of abuse, the uncertainty of my stay in the United States, and the rejection and betrayal of the people I trusted the most. But my purpose kept me from throwing in the towel.

Life can overwhelm us at times, but the one thing that can give us the strength to pull through is our purpose. The clearer your purpose, the stronger it will be to pull you through life's challenges. If you are certain about your purpose for living, you would endure life's challenges knowing that nothing can trump your purpose. In other words, if you know your "why" for living, you can endure just about any "how."

When the angel of the Lord told Mary that she was going to have a son named Jesus, she asked the angel, "How shall this be, seeing that I know not a man?" (Luke 1:34 KJV). The angel explained to Mary that she would be overshadowed by the Spirit of the Most High God.

This verse reminds us that how we will fulfill our purpose is not our responsibility—so we need to quit wasting our mental energy worrying about it. The responsibility of how we fulfill our purpose is the responsibility of the One who gave it to us. The Spirit of God in you will orchestrate the "how" once you figure out the "why." Now, this is not to say you shouldn't be strategic. Once you discover your purpose, you ought to be intentional about the things you do thereafter. No matter what you decide to do, don't lose sight of your purpose. Let your purpose drive your actions.

Priscilla Shirer—a phenomenal speaker, Bible teacher, and author—added acting to her portfolio when she starred in the faith-based movie, War Room. Though her role in the movie came as a surprise to many, in one of her interviews she explained that the reason she accepted the part was that it aligned with her purpose. She realized the movie wasn't a departure from what she already does, it was only a different expression of what she does. She realized the movie would be delivering the same message that she would want to deliver anyway. The movie was just another medium for ministry, which aligns with her purpose to strengthen the body of Christ.

Your purpose will always push you to do things you never thought possible. You were made to live a life of contribution. Commit to living beyond yourself. God has equipped you for a specific assignment and it's your responsibility to find out what that assignment is.

Habakkuk 2:2 (NKJV) says, "Write the vision and make it plain on tablets, that he may run who reads it."

God is saying to us: Chase after destiny. Destiny is the life that lies ahead of you. But you can only fulfill your destiny when you are in alignment with God's purpose for your life. When you do discover your purpose, you ought to write it down in ink on paper. It's not enough to know your purpose by heart. You've got to take a step further by writing it in plain language. A written word is powerful. A written word is a living word. Jesus overcame Satan in the wilderness by the written Word of God. You cannot refer to something that is not written. We can quote the words of people who inspire us because their works were written in the form of books. We can quote the Bible because it is written.

If we fail to write out our purpose, then before long we will lose sight of it. When our purpose is written and placed where we can see it every day, recitation becomes inevitable. Recitation of your purpose will imprint your purpose on your heart and consequently, in your mind and spirit. At this point, wherever you go, your purpose goes with you. You begin to run with it. You dream about it when you sleep, and you wake up with ideas on how to pursue it. You chase after your destiny by acting on your purpose.

The anchor scripture of my purpose is found in Isaiah 61:1 (NKJV) and it reads, "The Spirit of the Lord God is upon Me; because the Lord has anointed Me to preach good tidings to the poor; He has sent me to heal the brokenhearted, to proclaim liberty to the captives, and the opening of the prison to those who are bound." This is the reason I am living. I have this Bible verse boldly written on my bathroom wall and I recite it every day. God has uniquely gifted me with the skills I need to walk in my purpose. My speaking and writing skills are the channels with which I use to reach those who are wounded, broken, and hopeless.

When I decided to open up about my experience as a victim of domestic abuse, other women who were going through what I had been through were eager to know how I made it through my experience. Could it be that God is waiting for you to be open about your deepest hurts? That could be the gateway to your purpose.

Carrying all the weight from past hurts will prevent you from chasing destiny. Imagine trying to run with a heavy load on your shoulder. You are likely to quit running because of the weight of the load. Most of us are attempting to chase after destiny with so much weight and baggage from the past. The heavier you are, the harder it will be for you to run with the vision God has given you. You can only run with your vision when you are light.

Jesus is saying to you, "Come to me, all you who are weary and burdened, and I will give you rest. Take my yoke upon you, and learn of me, for I am gentle and humble in heart, and you will find rest for your souls. For my yoke is easy, and my burden is light" (Matthew 11:28-30 NIV).

We serve a God who is touched by our pain because He too was tempted in every way while He was on earth. He knows what it's like to be persecuted, abandoned, rejected, mocked, and abused—so we can trust and believe Him when He says He understands our pain.

You have a Father you can run to when you are in trouble. You have a God who is waiting with open arms to receive you.

Nothing is greater than our God. He can remove the weight from your shoulders, but you've got to be willing to surrender it all. You cannot fulfill your destiny without the One who created you.

It's time to get right with God. To give Him every part of you—withholding nothing. You are not in charge of your life, God is. All you are and all you will ever be is only by the grace of God. I shouldn't have survived what I went through, but the grace of God preserved me. When the enemy tried to snatch my life through physical and spiritual attacks, the blood of Jesus protected me.

I have realized that once you begin to chase after your destiny, all hell will break loose in your direction. The attacks you experience are designed to stop you from chasing your destiny. So, the attacks ought to get you excited because they are coming at you because of where you are headed. When I decided to pursue my dreams in spite of all the odds, I encountered unbelievable roadblocks. I received a lot of backlash from people, especially church folk who thought I shouldn't have left an abusive marriage. What they failed to realize is that the first thing anyone in a physically abusive relationship should do is to run for safety. You may not have the courage to report the abuse the moment it happens, but you can leave the scene of abuse even if it happens to be your home. Just because abuse happens in your bedroom doesn't make it any less of a crime. The danger of not leaving the scene of abuse is that you may never live to tell the story. Ultimately, you could be trading your destiny for a relationship that is headed for destruction.

After my separation, I got a one-bedroom apartment for myself, my son, and my mother. We had peace of mind until I decided to give my ex-husband another chance. I allowed him to move into my apartment when our son turned a year old, but the reconciliation was short lived. Soon after moving in, my ex-husband called the cops on my mother accusing her of assault. The cops found no evidence of his allegations and my mother was vindicated. But by this point, I was furious. I wasn't going to condone any form of disrespect against my mother. Any man who will not honor your mother is not worthy of being in your life. You can have another spouse, but you can never have another mother. The Bible says, "Honor your father and your mother, so that you may live long in the land the LORD your God is giving you" (Exodus 20:12 NIV). Your longevity here on earth is tied to the honor you give whoever represents mother and father in your life. All that I am today I owe to my mother. The same day my ex-husband attempted to dishonor my mother was the day I put him out of my apartment for good.

A few weeks later, I realized I was pregnant with our second child. I was so ashamed of being pregnant and separated, but I never lost sight of the life I could have if only I persevered. Your destiny is greater than what you are going through. So long as you have life in you, you can still chase after destiny. Chasing destiny means moving forward not going backward. You've come too far to return to where you used to be. Your future is ahead not behind you. What is behind cannot produce what lies ahead, but what you have today can birth your future.

What you have right now is valuable—don't despise it. When Jesus fed five thousand people with two fish and five loaves of bread, He used what little food was already there and multiplied it to feed the crowd (Matthew 14:19). When Jesus turned water into wine, He used what was available at the wedding to perform a miracle (John 2:8-9). When Moses stretched his hand over the Red Sea at God's command, the waters parted (Exodus 14:21). David had only five smooth stones and a slingshot, but that was enough to kill a giant (1 Samuel 17:40).

In the same vein, God is going to use what you've got right now to bless you. Quit looking at the past for miracles and choose to be present in this moment right now. The miracle you need lies in what you have in your hand. God knows that what you have left is all you need to make it happen. God will use the job you have right now to open greater opportunities of elevation for you. God will use the gifts He has given you to usher you into great places. God will use your cognitive abilities to create the life you've always wanted. God will use your artistic abilities to bless your life. God will use the virtues you have to preserve your generation.

Whatever you possess, the Lord can use for His glory. What you have left is what God will use to bless you. I believe you can recover what you've lost in the past if you don't despise what you've got right now. You will recover all you've lost when you put what you've got to use. Cherish what you have left. Cherish your gifts. Cherish your family. Cherish the people God has placed in your life. Cherish every moment.

There were times when I failed to live in the moment and

all I wanted was the next big thing. I urge you to snap out of that mentality. You can only chase destiny by living in the moment.

Discovering your purpose and working to fulfill your destiny will certainly invade your space. No one can answer the call of destiny without first giving themselves over to something greater. Destiny is not selfish—it is selfless. Destiny says you are the instrument, not the focal point; others are. You must learn to think less of yourself and more of others.

Those who are pursuing their destiny are global thinkers, not local thinkers. They let their minds stretch far beyond their present circumstance. They are consumed by their purpose all day long. You've got to be obsessed with your purpose and the pursuit of it. Remember your purpose is the reason God put you on this earth. God created you to serve Him first and your purpose next (Psalms 2:11). Your purpose is what you are living for. You cannot find your purpose and remain the same. Your purpose will empower you to do the things you wouldn't do ordinarily. Most people say they want to live an extraordinary life, but they don't want the challenges that come along with it.

Personally, I like to work behind the scenes where I can conceal my performance and remain anonymous. I'm comfortable so long as I'm not in the spotlight. The only problem with this is that my purpose has been designed to put me out there. Sharing my personal story is invading my space. I never wanted to share my story, but my purpose demands that I do so. Sharing my story puts my business out there for everyone to see. But at the same time, it restores the people I have been called to reach.

Once again, this is not a selfish game; it's a selfless one. Purpose is like a floodlight that shines not only on your life but on everything within its reach. Refusing to reveal your true self will suppress your purpose and deny your destiny of its full potential. Your purpose is designed to stretch you beyond your current limitations. That is where growth happens. Invasion leads to expansion. Therefore, if you want to expand your reach in life, you must be willing to be invaded. Your personal space cannot coexist with your purpose. One must give way to the other, and your purpose is worth taking up your personal space.

Some people aren't growing in life because they have decided to play safe, and you can't afford to live that way. You've got to be reckless about your purpose. People who play safe don't go far in life. Dare to allow your purpose to invade your space and watch your life turn into a miracle. Don't let your personal preferences drive the choices you make, but rather, let your purpose drive all that you do.

Your personal preferences are limited to the things you prefer and are comfortable with—and they could sabotage your destiny. You could be shutting off the people with whom you have common goals, simply because they don't appeal to your personal preferences. You cannot only be friends with those you "like" and those who do the things that appeal to you. That's not how you grow. You've got to be willing to associate with people who make you uncomfortable. If everyone in your circle is looking up to you for help, then you need to find new people who will challenge you to grow beyond where you are. Learn to get into circles where you feel the most uncomfortable. Learn to do the things that are outside the norm for you. That is exactly how you will grow and expand your thinking.

I wasn't open about my experience from the beginning. I tried to conceal my divorce in every way possible, but I felt constricted each time I had to do that. I found myself avoiding speaking in public because I was afraid of the personal questions people could ask me. But when I began to realize my fear was actually swallowing up my gift of public speaking, I decided to quit being worried about what other people thought about me. To protect my gift, I had to risk being vulnerable.

The invasion of destiny brings about vulnerability. You cannot be guarded and have destiny flow through you. You've got to let your walls down. You've got to allow yourself to flow like a river. You've got to be transparent, reckless, and vulnerable. Destiny invades your space, but it frees your spirit. And I would much rather have a free spirit than a guarded life. When we close ourselves up, nothing is able to go into us and nothing can come out. Before long, we will become stagnant if we stay closed. But when we are open, virtues are able to flow in and out of us.

Since I decided to allow destiny to invade my space, my life has been enriched in so many ways. I am learning more about myself, I am allowing people to pour into me, and I am better equipped to pour into others. You've been called to impact others, but you can only lead people as far as you've gone yourself. I have had a few women reach out to me for counsel after they heard my story and I have come to realize that most women are more comfortable talking about their failed relationships than they are about discussing domestic abuse (especially if they are victims). They are often ashamed to let people know that the same man they have showcased in public as their lover is physically abusing them.

Feelings of guilt and shame are from the enemy. The Bible dismisses every form of shame in the following verses: "Anyone who believes in Him will never be put to shame" (Romans 10:11 NIV) and "For there is no difference between Jew and Gentile—the same Lord is Lord of all and richly blesses all who call on him, for everyone who calls on the name of the Lord will be saved" (Romans 10:12-13 NIV).

We must live as though we believe there is no condemnation for those who belong to Christ Jesus. You are redeemed from every bit of shame and guilt over your life. So, square your shoulders, hold your head up, and walk like you've been redeemed.

Some fear how they would survive without the provision of their abuser when their abuser is their spouse. If they have children with their abuser, they feel obligated to remain in the abusive relationship. I had all these fears as well, but the thought of what could become of me if I remained in the abusive relationship stirred me to change. Chances were, if I stayed, I could end up bitter and resentful. If I stayed, I could become mentally unstable. If I stayed, I would likely ruin my life and the lives of my children and family. Worse yet, if I stayed—I knew there was a possibility I could lose my life. All of these likely outcomes made me realize that my life was worth preserving.

You cannot be under the same roof with an abuser and hope they wake up one morning completely changed without help. I hate to be the bearer of bad news, but that is not going to happen. Your life is worth preserving and anyone who chooses to destroy it must be deserted. Stand up for yourself. Reach out for help and expose any form of abuse before it swallows you whole. Destiny is on your life and it has come to invade your space.

3
THE PROCESS

It is important to know that not everyone will understand your purpose or the call of God upon your life. The moment you discover your purpose in life is the moment you will begin to encounter resistance from the people around you. Purpose will cause you to function differently from what others consider normal. Once this group of people sees the difference in your life, they are likely to oppose your new way of living. Oppositions will come in form of mockery, rejection, jealousy, and even hatred.

When Jesus was here on earth, He encountered resistance from people who thought He wasn't the Son of God. But when Jesus was being persecuted by these people, He prayed, "Father, forgive them for they do not know what they are doing" (Luke 23:24 NIV). Jesus understood that people will mock what they don't understand. You cannot allow the mockery of a few people get you off course. You've got to do as Jesus did: pray for them and keep moving. You don't have to come up with a comeback or "clapback," as the millennials would say. You don't have to waste your time responding to everyone's opinion of you. You don't have to spend time trying to get everyone to understand your purpose. Just be authentic and everyone else will adjust. Remember talk is cheap, so let them talk. Do the uncommon thing and do what others wouldn't do. Most people try to have the last word in every argument, but you don't have time for that. You have a higher calling on your life.

I have come to realize: the more distinct you are from others, the more sought after you will be. If the identity and purpose of Jesus were questioned, and if we are modeling our lives after Him, then we shouldn't expect to go through life without being questioned, misunderstood, mocked, envied, and even hated.

The story of Joseph, starting in Genesis Chapter 37, is a fitting example of what we are likely to experience on our road to destiny. Joseph was mocked by his brothers for being a dreamer. His brothers didn't understand the plan of God for his life and as such, they were very envious of him. Their envy for Joseph led them to sell him as a slave.

It's one thing for people to dislike you, but it's completely another when those people are your family members. It's twice as painful when those close to you are the ones who hurt and betray you.

Many people will agree with you, so long as you stay within the parameters they are accustomed to. Once you step out of those parameters, they become threatened by your courage to pursue something greater. Some people have decided to never leave the confines of their comfort zone because of fear, so they feel threatened when someone else decides to go for the same thing they have decided not to pursue.

Do you see why you cannot afford to be stopped by people who have decided not to want more out of life? When people oppose you, it's really not about you. Their attitude toward you stems from the insecurities they have yet to deal with within their own lives.

When Bishop T.D Jakes started his ministry, some people said he wasn't going to last very long. But he wasn't troubled by the mockery of his haters because he was grounded in his purpose. The people who mocked him didn't understand the calling on his life, but today everyone who knows who he is—including his critics—and all can attest to the fact that he is doing exactly what he is called to do. Through his ministry, Bishop Jakes has changed the lives of countless people, including mine.

Your purpose is greater than all your haters put together. The call of God upon your life is stronger than the opinions of men. Learn to rise above your haters, critics, and opposers by pushing the ignore button. You don't have to respond to them—simply ignore them. Become comfortable with not having everyone's endorsement. Become comfortable with resistance because that's how you grow and become better. Don't count on the cheers from others; instead, learn to count on you.

You are responsible for the outcome of your life. We all need encouragement from time to time, but sometimes you've got to do as David did in 1 Samuel 30:6 and encourage yourself. Be your own cheerleader. Don't carry a long face all day simply because some people aren't responding to you the way you want them to. Trust me, if you stay on track and refuse to be distracted, people will become drawn to the brightness of your light. Your light will soon invade the territories you have been assigned to conquer.

LEARN TO LOVE YOURSELF

You are the light of the world (Matthew 5:14). You hold the solution others are looking for, so you've got to treat yourself with care. Choosing to love yourself is the greatest gift you could ever give to yourself. Loving yourself is loving God because you're an express image of God.

When Jesus was asked what the greatest commandment was He responded, "Thou shalt love the Lord thy God with all thy heart, and with all thy soul, and with all thy mind. This is the first and greatest commandment. And the second is like unto it, thou shalt love thy neighbor as thyself" (Matthew 22:36-39 KJV). Therefore, loving God means loving your neighbor just as you love yourself. We cannot claim to love God when we don't love ourselves and those around us.

So often we find other people more talented and more attractive than ourselves, and if we aren't careful, we gradually begin to dislike ourselves for no reason at all. We could easily wish to have the personality of Adam, the appearance of Eve, the wealth of Solomon, the strength of Samson, and the heart of David—what a perfect combination that would be! We seem to want bits and pieces of what others have because, in all reality, no one has it all. We are all flawed human beings, though some people do appear to have it all together because they are confident in who they are. They believe they are enough, and so are you.

Knowing you are loved unconditionally by your Father in heaven is the greatest feeling in the world. Nothing compares to it. You don't need anyone's validation to understand that you are enough. You already have the right physical appearance, personality, and talents to fulfill your destiny. It can be very easy to think, if we had more of this or less of that, we would be successful. But I have great news for you: Nothing you could ever obtain can be more valuable than what you already have—and that's you.

You are irreplaceable. You are one of a kind. There has never been anyone like you and there will never be anyone like you. You cannot be replicated nor duplicated. No one in the world has your fingerprints. No one else can do the things you do in the same way you do them.

Loving yourself is food to your soul. You get to live confidently when you love yourself. Each time you look in the mirror, behold the wonder of God's creation. Loving yourself just the way you are will inspire you to reach higher and hope for better. Love is active. When you love yourself, you give to yourself. You adopt lifestyle changes that express your love for you. And as you take care of yourself, you naturally become a more confident individual.

Discipline is one of the many benefits of a lifestyle change. Discipline is what separates the talkers from the doers. You can talk about your goals for as long as you want, but nothing will change until you begin to take action. It takes discipline to commit to living a life of excellence. It takes discipline to pursue your dreams. It takes discipline to demand more out of yourself every day. It takes discipline to do the things that strengthen your body, mind, soul, and spirit.

Your body is the only place you have to live in and you owe it to yourself to take care of it. If your health is threatened due to negligence, you could run the risk of not fulfilling your own destiny. Don't just wish you were athletic—begin training like an athlete. Don't just wish you were a better communicator—practice becoming a better communicator. Don't just wish you had more friends—start working on becoming a more lovable person. Don't just wish you could write a book—start putting your thoughts on paper every day. Anything you feed will certainly grow and whatever you starve will eventually die. Feed yourself with love, peace, grace, mercy, knowledge, and discipline and watch your life evolve.

I was listening to one of Tyler Perry's interviews and he mentioned how Oprah Winfrey inspired him to put his thoughts on paper. Eventually, his thoughts were transformed into scripts for plays and movies. Tyler started writing plays when no one knew him as the entertainment mogul he now is. Tyler had a very rough start in the entertainment business, but he never gave up. He trusted in the scripts he had written and after several years of trying to promote his idea, he had a breakthrough.

Tyler's story goes to show how powerful our words are. Words are living things. Our thoughts are magnified when we capture them on paper. I can attest to this because when I decided to write this book, I wasn't sure if I had enough life experience to create an entire book. However, each time I wrote one word, I was inspired to add more words to make sentences, more sentences to make paragraphs, and eventually, many paragraphs to fill pages.

The first draft of the movie Rocky was written by Sylvester Stallone in only three days. The movie has earned over $225 million from global box office sales. Rocky was a hit, winning three Oscars, ranking as one of the world's greatest sports movies, and has had six sequels since 1976 when it was first made. Though we know the movie's success now, Sylvester Stallone was living in a desperate situation when he wrote the first script. He faced many rejections from possible movie producers, but he never gave up. Stallone even turned down several offers for the film that required another actor for the main role because he wanted to star in the movie as Rocky. Eventually, Sylvester was offered a paltry sum to be featured in the movie and he accepted. People thought he had lost his mind, but little did they know, the movie was going to become a huge hit. Sylvester's life turned around in one moment because he wrote down the thoughts he held in his mind.

You don't have to know the outcome of your dream before you proceed; you just have to trust your instinct. You cannot afford to play it safe in life. It's too risky not to take a risk. And when you do take a risk, trust that you have made the right decision for yourself. Even when the outcome is not desirable, don't stop trying. You could be on the brink of a breakthrough, but you can only have the breakthrough if you don't quit.

DON'T SEEK MAN, SEEK THE ANOINTING

Acceptance is a need everyone desperately seeks. But in reality, you cannot be accepted by everyone and you've got to be okay with that. After Jesus commissioned his disciples to go into cities and proclaim the gospel, He warned them about rejection saying, "If anyone will not welcome you or listen to your words, leave that home or town and shake the dust off your feet" (Matthew 10:14, NIV). Jesus knew they wouldn't be accepted wherever they went, but He told them exactly what to do when that happened, and He is saying the same thing to you today: When people fail to accept you, shake the dust off your feet and keep moving.

When you have been called by God, you don't need the approval of men. When Jesus called the twelve disciples, He gave them the power to cast out demons and heal all manner of diseases. In the same vein, God has called you for a specific assignment and He has also equipped you with the power to carry out your assignment. So, you don't need people to validate the power of God at work within you. Quit trying to explain yourself to everyone simply because you want to gain their approval. Their approval isn't needed. The people you have been called to touch will receive you when you show up.

When you are anointed for your assignment, you've got to be ready for resistance. **The anointing upon your life is both defensive and offensive. It protects, and it provokes. It heals, and it destroys. It blesses, and it curses. It crushes, and it restores.** Carrying an anointing from God is not for the faint of heart. The anointing will give you the boldness you need to operate in the area you have been called to function. But, if you step out of your assignment in an attempt to please people, you will lose the protective covering of the anointing. The anointing will not serve the flesh; it will only honor the spirit.

Your assignment is given to you by God alone. You don't get to choose what, where, or how you want it to be. You are chosen by God to represent Christ, not man. When

King Nebuchadnezzar confronted Shadrach, Meshach, and Abednego in Daniel Chapter 3 about their refusal to worship the golden image he had set up, they answered him saying, "King, O Nebuchadnezzar, we are not careful to answer thee in this matter" (Daniel 3:16 KJV). What they were saying was that they were unapologetic about who they were called to be. The king could throw them into a burning furnace if he wanted to, but they knew the God they served would deliver them.

When the anointing is at work, you become fearless, even in the face of death. The anointing consumes every fear of opposition. When the king heard the unapologetic words coming from Shadrach, Meshach, and Abednego, he demanded that the furnace be heated seven times hotter. The king was offended by the anointing they carried, but the three friends were still protected in the flames.

The fire was so hot that it burned the men who threw them into it, but Shadrach, Meshach, and Abednego came out of the fire completely unscathed. Scriptures tell us that they didn't even smell like smoke (Daniel 3:27)! That is the mystery of the anointing. It slays some and protects others. It's not your job to explain to people what the Lord is doing in you and through you. The anointing will draw close the people who are called to be in your circle and repel those who aren't. The anointing will bring the right people to you without coercion.

Quit seeking acceptance and start seeking the anointing. The anointing gets you battle ready. David fought and killed Goliath after he was anointed to be king by Samuel (1 Samuel

16). There are battles in your life that you won't be able to fight until you are anointed. David was so certain he would defeat the giant that he approached Goliath to fight him. When you are anointed for an assignment, you don't wait to be reminded what to do—you do so intuitively. You don't turn your back on your assignment, you approach it and you get it done.

When God called me to write this book, I was tempted to give excuses as to why I couldn't do it. I was afraid of being vulnerable about my past, but the anointing is what shattered my fear. I began to realize that my freedom was tied to my obedience to do what God was asking me to do. You are the most powerful when you are walking in obedience and pursuing the call of God upon your life. Nothing matters more than this.

I am unapologetic for answering the call of God upon my life. I am unapologetic for receiving the never-ending love of God. I am unapologetic for receiving the unconditional love of my husband. I am unapologetic for refusing to stay in a relationship that was designed to destroy my destiny. I am unapologetic for choosing to raise my children in the fear of the Lord. I am unapologetic for choosing to walk in honor and integrity. I am unapologetic for choosing me.

I love myself, and I urge you to love yourself too.

Choose to love yourself, despite the mistakes and poor decisions you have made. Choose to love yourself, despite the flaws you have. Choose to love the good, the bad, and the ugly—and watch the power of your decision unfold.

THE POWER OF YOUR DECISION

The only person you will become is the person you decide to become; not the person you wish to become, and certainly not the person others have said you will become.

If you haven't decided to become successful, there is a 100 percent chance that you won't be. If you are going to get ahead in life, then you have got to decide to get ahead. After a year and half of domestic abuse, I decided I wasn't going to continue to live with an abuser as a husband. Had I not made that decision, the abuse would have continued, and I never would have experienced the life I now have.

The turning point began the moment I decided to put an end to the abuse. Your decision will determine your outcome in life. This book is only a reality because I decided to write it. Think about anything you've ever accomplished in life. You had to decide to do it and that's why you did. **Decision precedes action.** Without the decision to pursue your dreams, you will not take the necessary steps needed to make it a reality. In simple terms, if you don't decide to make apple pie for dinner, you won't look up the recipe or attempt to make it. Until you decide to become successful, you will not have the motivation to study success.

Some people go through life wishing and hoping things will get better and they end up not accomplishing anything because they are either too weak or too indecisive to determine who they want to become. In life, you must determine who you want to become, and if you fail to decide, then you've decided to become nothing. Don't let anyone fool you, indecision is a decision. If you've ever taken a multiple-choice test before, you would agree that the instructions usually state to select the answer you consider correct for each question. This means you must select an answer from the multiple-choices listed, and if you don't, then you will fail the test.

The same applies to life. When you fail to decide to succeed in life, you are simply saying it's okay to fail. Not being able to decide on something is an act of weakness. Weak people are experts at this. They can't seem to make a decision. They would rather sit on the fence where they think they are safe. They are often spectators in life, they criticize others, they are insecure, and they lack confidence in themselves. They are often resentful because they have regrets stemming from their indecision. They refer to successful people as crooks and usually, they will not amount to very much in life.

If we are going to become all that God has intended for us to become, then we must decide to become more than we are right now. It all begins with a decision. When your mind is made up on something, nothing can stop you. Anything that attempts to stop you will be crushed by the intensity of your resolve. That's how powerful your decisions are!

To make sound decisions, you need the help of the Holy Spirit—the spirit that lives on the inside of you. That's the spirit that guides you. Zechariah 4:6 (NIV) is very clear on the power of the Holy Spirit saying, "Not by might nor by power but by my Spirit, says the Lord Almighty." We cannot become who we were created to be without the help of the Holy Spirit. The Holy Spirit is our helper (John 14:16) and only He can teach us what we need to do in order to become who God has called us to be. If we are open to His counsel and grant Him full access into our lives, He will teach us great and mighty things.

I had an incredible encounter with the Holy Spirit a few years ago, just before Easter Sunday. That week, I went to pick up my oldest child from daycare and the daycare administrator handed me a bouquet of fresh palm frond to take home with me. The delicate branches smelled so fresh, and I placed them in a tall vase of water as soon as I got home.

While I was praying that night, the Lord began to show me how similar we are to the palm frond. A palm frond cannot survive outside of the palm tree because the tree carries the life that the palm frond needs. In the same way, we cannot survive without God because in Him is everlasting life. If God abides in us and we abide in Him, we will have life without end. There is no life outside of Him. He is the vine and we are the branches (John 15:5). In Him we live and move and have our being (Acts 17:28).

Sometimes, when we catch a glimpse of where God is taking us, we take off running only to end up in places we least expect. When we are separated from God, we are cut off from the source of life. When we are disconnected from God, we begin to make choices that are born out of our own desires and not out of the will of God.

My previous marriage was outside the perfect will of God for my life. My decision to marry my ex-husband was born out of my own sinful desire. Yet, God being so merciful, used my mistake to draw me back to Himself. The collapse of my previous marriage opened my eyes to see how much God loved me. I couldn't see the mess I was in until I got out of it.

A few years after my divorce, my mother showed me photographs I had taken of myself when I was married, and I didn't even recognize myself. I looked lost and confused in the pictures. There was no sparkle in my eyes. I shouldn't have survived the consequences of my decision, but only by the grace of God, I did.

I was like the palm frond that was cut off from the palm tree that gave it life. The bouquet of palm fronds sitting on my kitchen counter, as beautiful as they looked, would shrink and die in a matter of hours if taken out of the water. When we fail to immerse ourselves in the living water of God's Word, we shrink and eventually die spiritually. For us to remain green and fresh, we must stay grounded in the living Word of God. God's Word is the living water and the Bible records in John 1:1 (NIV), "In the beginning was the Word, and the Word was with God, and the Word was God." Therefore, the Word of God is God Himself. We may not see God face to face, but we can encounter Him through His Word.

Psalm 1:1-3 (NKJV) says, "Blessed is the man who walks not in the counsel of the ungodly, nor stands in the path of sinners, nor sits in the seat of the scornful; But his delight is in the law of the Lord, and in His law he meditates day and night. He shall be like a tree planted by the rivers of water, that brings forth fruit in his season, his leaf will not wither and whatsoever he does shall prosper." If you want to stay green and fresh, then you must have the Word of God in you. Having the word of God in you means constantly reading and studying the Bible. Just as rain waters the earth and causes the plants to grow and flourish, so does your soul need water (the Word of God) to produce fruit. Without the Word inside of us, we would dry up like a plant without water.

The Word of God is God Himself. No wonder Jesus, while speaking to the Samaritan woman in John 4:14, referred to the water He gives as eternal. "But whosoever drinks of the water that I shall give him will never thirst; but the water that I shall give him will become in him a fountain of water springing up into everlasting life" (John 4:14, NKJV). Jesus is the cup that will never run dry.

You cannot become the person you were called to be without the One who called you. When you decide to answer the call of God upon your life, you give up your ways for God's ways. God's ways may be unpopular, and they are often contradictory to the ways of the world. But when you commit to following God's ways, you will gradually become very effective at what you do. You will become the chosen and most preferred candidate everywhere you go.

I have experienced this in my own life. I have spoken certain things into reality and they happened just like I declared they would. I recall going for a job interview where I told myself I was going to have a conversation and not an interview with the interviewer. I arrived, and the interviewer liked me instantly. We had a wonderful conversation, just like I declared we would, and all she kept saying was, "You are too qualified for this position." I only had three months of experience in the area I was applying for, so in all reality, I had little to no experience. But the Lord made me the most preferred candidate for the job.

I love Newton's third law of motion that states: For every action, there is an equal and opposite reaction. I am not a physicist, but this law can be applied to the life of anyone who chooses to see more goodness and mercy in their life. Whatever we put out into the universe is exactly what we get back. Our input will always determine our output. The energy we put out is what we will get back. If you smile at people, people will smile back at you. If you are nice to people, people will be nice to you. If you forgive people easily, you will be forgiven too. If people are constantly frowning at you, check your own attitude. It is often said: A bad attitude is like a flat tire; you can't go anywhere until you change it. A change in attitude could be all there is to the unpleasant responses you are receiving from those around you.

Galatians 6:7 (NKJV) says, "Do not be deceived; God cannot be mocked, for whatsoever a man sows, that he will also reap." There could not be a more true statement than this: Everyone will reap what they sow. If you don't like the fruit you are producing, then start sowing different seeds. You cannot plant cactus seeds and expect to reap apples. That's impossible! The exciting and frightening thing about sowing and reaping is that you get to reap whatever you sow in abundance. I have never seen an apple tree that bears only one apple. An apple tree produces apples in abundance. The same is true about poison ivy seeds. We've got to be very careful about the seeds we sow because, in due time, we will reap the abundance of what we have sown.

It is against the law of nature for a person to reap where

they have not sown. In other words, you cannot make a withdrawal where you haven't made a deposit. When you attempt to reap where you haven't sown, you become a robber. Life will fight against anyone who attempts to go against the principle of sowing and reaping. The principle of sowing and reaping will happen irrespective of what we do. No wonder the Bible says, "As long as the earth endures, seedtime and harvest, cold and heat, summer and winter, day and night will never cease" (Genesis 8:22 NIV). This explains why we don't pray about certain things, and they happen anyway. It's the seed you have sown that is producing the outcome you are experiencing. Remember, those that sow in tears will reap in joy (Psalms 126:5), so it's in our best interest to sow good seeds.

Seeds, when planted, will eventually sprout and cover an entire field of land. It only takes one good seed to yield an abundant harvest. But here's the formula for an abundant harvest in life: sow generously, sow in love, sow with joy, and sow in faith. Sowing is what guarantees your harvest in life. It's impossible for anyone to experience harvest without first sowing a seed. This is not a curse; it is an irrevocable law of nature instituted by God Himself. The principle of sowing and reaping can be applied in any area of our lives, especially in wealth creation.

After my divorce, I struggled with my finances. Raising my children and working a fulltime job, with little or no child support, was a struggle, to say the least. I knew there had to be a better way to live than to struggle with my finances month after month. Then, I came across an audiobook entitled, The Richest Man in Babylon by George S. Clason. In my opinion, this is one of the most inspiring books on wealth ever written. It talks in part about the seven cures to a lean purse. One of which, is to make your coins multiply. The writer says, "Put each coin to laboring that it may reproduce its kind even as flocks of the field and help to bring to thee income, a stream of wealth that shall flow constantly into thy purse."

This principle is profound. Everything we sow must multiply. We can only have multiplication when we have invested in something profitable. This sounds like common knowledge, but not common practice. If we all practiced this principle, we would have more wealthy people in the world today. What we believe about wealth determines how much of it we can create because wealth is a mentality.

Deuteronomy 8:18 (NIV) says, "But remember the Lord your God, for it is He who gives you the ability to produce wealth…" In other words, wealth is created through the power that lies within us. For a man to create wealth, he must first believe that the power to do so lies within him. He must program his mind to think in terms of wealth and not lack. His mind must first believe that it possesses the power to create wealth. Your wealth is determined by the level of your creativity. The more creative you are, the wealthier you will become.

Now, here's my own definition of wealth: **Wealth is the creative power that lies within every man that refuses to acknowledge lack.** To a wealthy person, lack doesn't exist. They have a mentality that believes everything is in abundance. Think about it. Everything that God created is in abundance: the trees, the animals, the land, the sea.

Everything was created in abundance. Therefore, wealth can only be yours when you think in terms of abundance. This is what separates the haves from the have-nots. The haves believe they can create anything they desire, and they do. On the other hand, the have-nots do not believe that they can have abundance, so they don't.

Wealth is not limited to how much money you have in the bank; rather, it is the mentality that knows no limitation. I have studied a myriad of wealthy individuals and almost all of them came from lowly backgrounds. The stories are all the same: They didn't have much to work with, but they had a mentality that refused to accept limitation. They were never limited to the circumstances they found themselves in, and thus, their minds went to work and created the wealth they knew was possible to possess.

After my divorce, life was tough. My children and I didn't have much, but my mind refused to accept lack. I refused to accept that being a single parent was synonymous with poverty. I refused to accept that wealth was only for a few lucky people. I never expected anyone to hand to me what I knew I could provide for myself. I never saw my children as a burden; instead, I embraced the responsibility of being a parent. I never saw myself as destitute. I knew I was called to be a lender and not a borrower.

When I was living in a one-bedroom apartment, my mentality was not confined to the four small walls of the building. I often saw myself in lofty places, and I knew I could create that mental picture in my life. I realized I was the only one who could create the life I desired to have.

You determine the wealth you enjoy in life through your own creativity. Creativity simply means the ability to solve problems. The more problems you are willing to solve, the more wealth you can create for yourself. When I understood this about wealth, I knew there was no limit to the abundance I could experience. I knew I wasn't going to work a job until I reach the age of retirement. I knew I could experience a life of abundance.

4
A GIVING MENTALITY

If you are going to enjoy the life God has given you, then you've got to learn to be a giver. Luke 6:38 (NIV) says, "Give, and it will be given to you. A good measure, pressed down, shaken together and running over, will be poured into your lap. For with the measure you use, it will be measured to you." This is not to say you shouldn't enjoy receiving gifts when they are offered, it is simply stating that it is more blessed to give than to receive.

We have been called to give from the abundance that God has given to us. To a giver, nothing is in short supply. So often, we tie giving to money; however, your giving is not limited to your financial resources. You could give your time to the things of the Kingdom. You could give words of encouragement to the brokenhearted. You could give your energy to serve your family and the people you come across. You could give your talent to be used in the area God has called you. You could give your resources to support good causes that you feel passionate about. The list is endless.

Nature detests people who only want to take and not give back. The most memorized scripture of all time is John 3:16 (NIV) and it says, "For God so loved the world that He gave His only begotten son, that whoever believes in Him should not perish but have eternal life." Until we can give freely of what we have received from God, we may never experience the abundance of God's blessings.

Giving is a supernatural law that guarantees the good measure, pressed down, and shaken together of the blessings we have been promised. When we are generous, God places us in charge of plenty. He opens greater resources to us knowing we can be trusted. Your prosperity is not tied to your prayer; rather, it is tied to your giving. Bishop David Oyedepo once said, "You don't pray your way into prosperity—you give your way into prosperity." And that is so true! The secret to becoming prosperous is reckless giving. Anyone can be prosperous because we all have something to give. Use what you've got to produce more resources for yourself.

So, what are you willing to give up in exchange for what you want? Put differently, what sacrifice are you willing to make to achieve what you want? You've got to make up your mind to pay the cost of what you desire to have. It's impossible to achieve your desires without sacrifice. Something has got to give! For me, I had to give up the habits that were preventing me from moving forward in life. The need to appear perfect in the eyes of everyone around me was a major hindrance for me. For a while, I didn't want anyone to see my brokenness. I was too ashamed to admit that my previous marriage didn't work. Even after my divorce, I refused to take responsibility for the choices I had made that contributed to the demise of my marriage. I had a perfect picture of how my life ought to look, and I made sure I covered up anything that tainted that image.

The problem with my picture was, it was totally my idea and not God's. What I thought was a wise thing to do, was foolishness in

God's eyes. **Until you are willing to risk being foolish before men, you cannot receive all that God has in store for you.** I have learned to give up my intelligence for God's wisdom. I have learned to give up my past for my glorious future. Giving up the fear of being judged by my past allowed me to forgive myself, and to embrace the life I have (not the one I wish I had). You can't receive freedom until you let go of what is holding you down. I let go of my past and God gave me exactly what I needed for the fulfillment of my purpose.

ONLY LIGHT CAN EXPEL DARKNESS

In the beginning, the Bible records that darkness covered the face of the earth until God said, "Let there be light," and there was light (Genesis 1:3 NIV). Darkness will not bow to anything, except light. When a light bulb is switched on, darkness disappears immediately. That's how powerful the effect of light is. It never leaves you the same. Some people are experiencing darkness in their lives, and Jesus has called you and me to be the light of the world. Matthew 5:16 (NIV) says, "Let your light shine before others, that they may see your good deeds and glorify your Father in heaven." Light is the only thing that can expel darkness. Light brings revelation, and revelation brings understanding. We can contact light by studying the Word of God.

The Psalmist says, "Thy Word is a lamp unto my feet, and a light unto my path" (Psalms 119:105 KJV). The Word of God is light. If you want to see where you are going, then you must study the map. Dave Martin once said, "The difference between where you are now and where you are going is what you know." If you know better, you will live better. It's our responsibility to search and study for the things we desire to have. If you desire to be wealthy, then study wealth. If you desire to be a leader, then study leadership. Life is a journey, and if you are going to arrive at your destination then you must first look up where you are going. No one sets out on a journey without a map. If you do, you are most likely to wind up where you least expected.

Some people are so consumed by the shadow of the object they desire that they never behold the image that is casting the shadow. It's easy to become lazy and depend solely on what others have studied instead of studying for yourself. Life is too precious for anyone to go through without encountering light for themselves. The entrance of light gives understanding, but you cannot receive light unless you study it for yourself. **You can only get rid of ignorance by seeking knowledge.**

Study, so you can become the light that drives away darkness. Let the brightness of your light draw countless men and women to God. There's nothing more empowering than turning on a light bulb when and where you need it. Light reveals the truth and the truth is liberating. It doesn't matter how dark your season has been, I say to you: Arise and shine for your light has come.

Receive the Light of God as you read Isaiah 60:1-22 (NIV) today:
"Arise, shine, for your light has come,
and the glory of the LORD rises upon you.
See, darkness covers the earth

and thick darkness is over the peoples,
but the LORD rises upon you
and his glory appears over you.
Nations will come to your light,
and kings to the brightness of your dawn.
Lift up your eyes and look about you:
All assemble and come to you;
your sons come from afar,
and your daughters are carried on the hip.
Then you will look and be radiant,
your heart will throb and swell with joy;
the wealth on the seas will be brought to you,
to you the riches of the nations will come.
Herds of camels will cover your land,
young camels of Midian and Ephah.
And all from Sheba will come,
bearing gold and incense
and proclaiming the praise of the LORD.
All Kedar's flocks will be gathered to you,
the rams of Nebaioth will serve you;
they will be accepted as offerings on my altar,
and I will adorn my glorious temple.
Who are these that fly along like clouds,
like doves to their nests?
Surely the islands look to me;
in the lead are the ships of Tarshish,
bringing your children from afar,
with their silver and gold,
to the honor of the LORD your God,

the Holy One of Israel,
for he has endowed you with splendor.
Foreigners will rebuild your walls,
and their kings will serve you.
Though in anger I struck you,
in favor I will show you compassion.
Your gates will always stand open,
they will never be shut, day or night,
so that people may bring you the wealth of the nations—
their kings led in triumphal procession.
For the nation or kingdom that will not serve you
will perish;
it will be utterly ruined.
The glory of Lebanon will come to you,
the juniper, the fir and the cypress together,
to adorn my sanctuary;
and I will glorify the place for my feet.
The children of your oppressors will come bowing
before you;
all who despise you will bow down at your feet
and will call you the City of the LORD,
Zion of the Holy One of Israel.
Although you have been forsaken and hated,
with no one traveling through,
I will make you the everlasting pride
and the joy of all generations.
You will drink the milk of nations
and be nursed at royal breasts.
Then you will know that I, the LORD, am your Savior,

your Redeemer, the Mighty One of Jacob.
Instead of bronze I will bring you gold,
and silver in place of iron.
Instead of wood I will bring you bronze,
and iron in place of stones.
I will make peace your governor
and well-being your ruler.
No longer will violence be heard in your land,
nor ruin or destruction within your borders,
but you will call your walls Salvation
and your gates Praise.
The sun will no more be your light by day,
nor will the brightness of the moon shine on you,
for the LORD will be your everlasting light,
and your God will be your glory.
Your sun will never set again,
and your moon will wane no more;
the LORD will be your everlasting light,
and your days of sorrow will end.
Then all your people will be righteous
and they will possess the land forever.
They are the shoot I have planted,
the work of my hands,
for the display of my splendor.
The least of you will become a thousand,
the smallest a mighty nation.
I am the LORD;
in its time I will do this swiftly."

OVERCOMING FEAR

I arrived in the United States alone in 2009. I entered an unfamiliar territory without my family, but I carried big dreams within my heart. One of which was to become a writer. I was afraid no one knew who I was, and I wondered how I would ever promote my work if I started writing. Then, I realized I couldn't spend my time wondering how I would get my goals met, I just had to act on them.

Worrying will never get anything done. When you worry, you waste valuable time that could be used to get things moving in the right direction. When I realized this, I began to take small consistent steps toward my desired goal. Action will always push us forward; inaction will keep us grounded. **Thinking about a problem doesn't solve it, but acting on a well thought out solution can make all the difference.** I began to shift my thinking from what I didn't have to what I did have. I didn't have the means to promote my ideas, but I had control over what I did with my ideas. You will never have all you need at one time to make your dreams come true. When you do come short in an area, see that shortcoming as a qualification for where you are going rather than a disqualification keeping you where you are. Your limitation is what qualifies you for your expectation. Jesus didn't come for those who had it all figured out. He came for you and me—those who cannot make it without Him (Matthew 9:13).

God can use you, despite the limitations that might be evident in your life. In Exodus 4:10 (NIV), Moses tried to remind God of his limitations and why he was the least likely person to lead the children of Israel out of Egypt. "Moses said to the Lord, Pardon your servant, Lord. I have never been eloquent, neither in the past nor since you have spoken to your servant. I am slow of speech and tongue." What Moses didn't realize is that God is very masterful at using our limitations for His glory.

Just like Moses, I had a list of limitations that held me back from pursuing my dreams sooner than I did. I felt like an alien in a foreign country. I was concerned about what people thought of me until I realized it wasn't my job to manage other people's opinions. I was trying to talk myself out of doing what I knew I was called to do. I thought if I could just remain hidden in a little corner, then no one would notice me, and life would be just fine. Then I recognized that you will never know what you can do unless you try.

I was tempted several times to settle for a life of safety and mediocracy. After all, I didn't have a network of people to help me, so how was I supposed to rise into prominence? To add to my resume of disqualification, my name is very distinct, and I was very uncomfortable with the responses I got when I introduced myself in public. Some people questioned my origin, my appearance, my accent, and so on. I was hurt by all these interrogations, so I found myself avoiding group meetings as a way to protect myself.

The irony is, all the things I had listed as my limitations were the very things that put me in the place I am today. When God blesses you, no limitation can hold you back. When God blesses you, no man born of a woman can curse you. I love God's response to Moses when he presented his limitations. The Lord said to him, "Who gave human beings their mouths? Who makes them deaf or mute? Who gives them sight or makes them blind? Is it not I, the Lord? Now go; I will help you speak and will teach you what to say" (Exodus 4:11-12 NIV).

No matter what you have on your list of limitations, God can still use you for His glory. Your limitations are crushed before the unlimited nature of your God. God can use anything and anyone for His glory. It doesn't matter what your background looks like. If He can use me, He can certainly use you. You've got to step out in faith, even if your knees are wobbling in fear. Your dreams are stronger than your fears. It's often said that fear is nothing more than False Evidence Appearing Real. And that is so true! Fear is not real.

We all have been called to do something greater than ourselves. We have been called to change the world through our works. Unfortunately, some of us are not living up to our full potential because of fear. Fear is a powerful spirit that can immobilize you if you let it. Remember God has not given us the spirit of fear but of a sound mind (2 Timothy 1:7).

The difference between people who are living their dreams and those who are not is their attitude toward fear. The courageous act in spite of fear, while the fearful retreat in the face of fear. **Some think courage is the absence of fear, but I say, courage is doing the things that make you fearful over and over again.**

Don't overthink the process of what needs to be done, just do it! There's a famous quote by Ray Bradbury that says, "Jump off the cliff and grow your wings on the way down." That's how you become a champion in life! The more you do things that make you fearful, the less fearful you will be. That's exactly how you deal with fear. You attack fear with action. Take life head-on, you cannot afford to be a spectator. Be among the few people who make things happen.

Years ago, when I would think about my dream of becoming a best-selling author, the fear of not having the influence to make it happen would paralyze me. I had a mental picture of what I wanted, but I didn't have the courage to go for it. At that moment, I realized I didn't need influence to get started, but I did need to start in order to gain influence. No one ever starts off in life as a pro. Everyone starts off as an amateur. Art Williams sums it up this way: "Remember, before you can be great, you've got to be good. Before you can be good, you've got to be bad. But before you can even be bad, you've got to try."

Every winner I know started off as a loser. A winner is simply a loser who kept trying. No one likes to fail, but failure precedes success. You've got to learn how to fail to succeed. Failure is the quickest way to win. Everyone wants to win, but you learn more when you lose. Learn to fail forward. Each time you fail at something, you are knowingly or unknowingly taking a step closer to becoming a winner. As painful as losing may feel, it strengthens the core of who you are.

The area where you have experienced failure can become the area of your greatest strength if you choose to focus on the lessons rather than the pain. Often times, we can be so overwhelmed by the grief our failure caused that we miss the opportunity to learn from the lessons gained by the experience.

After the failure I experienced in my first marriage, I began to seek information on relationships. I had seen very successful marriages, so I knew it was possible to have one. I was hungry to know what makes a good, healthy relationship. I read every credible book I could find on marriage and relationships. As I invested in this area, I began to see the mistakes I had made in my own journey. Knowing what to do is fantastic but knowing what not to do can prevent a cycle of pain.

Let's face it, life is all about relationships. No one can live in isolation. It's not good for anyone to be alone. No matter how great your dreams are, you need people to help you accomplish them. Birthing your dream is like having a baby—and you cannot have a baby all by yourself. It doesn't matter how strong you are, you need a midwife to help you. In the same way, someone has to hold your hand as you birth your dream.

Some people have had a stillbirth because they refused to seek the help of a midwife. You cannot do life alone. You cannot prosper without people. We were created to complement each other. You can only be fruitful if you have meaningful relationships. And the most important relationship you will ever have with any other person is the one you have with your spouse. Pastor Mike Hayes once said, "Outside the God you choose to serve, the person you choose to marry can alter the course of your life forever." Before long, I began to have a clear picture of what it meant to be committed to another person other than myself.

There's a popular joke about bacon and eggs that is often

used to describe commitment: The next time you have bacon and eggs, remember that the chicken was involved, but the pig was committed. Yes! The pig laid it all down. That's exactly what commitment looks like. A lot of people want to be involved in something, but they don't want to be committed to anything. They like the finished product, but they don't want the process that produces the finished work—so they end up not accomplishing much in life. Such people are great at starting new things, but they lack the commitment to follow through. In the end, they have several abandoned projects without any finished work.

You want to be the person who is willing to lay it all down. The person who goes all the way. The person who starts and finishes their race. The person who never quits! The person who stays on course no matter what.

Commitment is fighting for what you want with all you have. There are no half-measures with commitment! It's all or nothing. Any marriage you see that is working is made up of two people who are completely committed to the well-being of the other. You want to have a spouse who is committed to creating a life with you, not someone who is just involved in making a baby with you.

If you want the best out of life, you must be willing to give all you have without any reservations. Life yields to people who are committed and relentless. Art Williams summed it up beautifully when he said, "All you can do is all you can do, and all you can do is enough. But be sure you do all you can do."

For a while, I thought that my dreams were too big to be accomplished, so I settled for safe. I knew I was called to use my voice to impact the world, but I didn't feel worthy of being used by God. This feeling made me shy away from opportunities that I should have taken advantage of. I was willing to pursue my dream, so long as it didn't put me on the spot. My turning point only came when I started asking myself hard, critical questions: How did I get here? Am I where I want to be in life? Where am I going? What am I doing every day in preparation for where I am going? What is holding me back from getting there? When I answered these questions for myself, I realized that I was nowhere close to where I wanted to be in life. I was overworked and underpaid. I was struggling financially. I knew I was living below my potential, and I wasn't happy about that.

If you summon the courage it takes to give honest answers to the questions above, your life will never be the same. The moment I decided to be brutally honest with myself was the moment I began to pursue my dreams intentionally.

If there is anything within you that feels there may be more to life than what you are experiencing right now, then there is. So often we know within ourselves that we can do more, but we get distracted by all the voices that tell us we can't. An African proverb says, "If there is no enemy within, the enemy without can do us no harm." The greatest war we will ever encounter is the one that goes on within our own minds.

The mind is a powerful tool that can either work for us or against us. We must train our minds to work for us by feeding ourselves edifying words, rather than those filled with negativity. Read, listen, speak out, and write words that align with what you want out of life. If done repeatedly, this simple practice has the power to change your entire life. You can rewrite a story of defeat, failure, and rejection by simply rewiring your mind. But rewiring your thinking is a daily practice, not a casual one. You must be intentional about what you want out of life. Life doesn't yield to people who are causal—it yields to those who are intentional, relentless, and purposeful.

Before you engage in any activity, always ask yourself: Is this productive? Would this activity draw me closer to my goals? If your answer is yes, then pursue the activity with all your might. Go after your dreams like your life depends on it—because it does. As the popular saying goes, "Work like your life depends on you and pray like it depends on God."

Remember faith without works is dead (James 2:17). This is where some people miss the mark. Your life is your responsibility, so quit blaming others for what happens to you. It would have been easy for me to sit back and blame my ex-husband for my condition, but I chose to take responsibility for my own life. Throwing pity parties and playing the blame game will only keep you defeated. Cowards blame others for their condition and you are not a coward. Arise and take charge of your life. Quit playing the role of a victim and start acting like the victor you are. Earl Nightingale said it best when he said, "Everyone is self-made, but only the successful will admit it." It doesn't matter what your life looks like right now, the good news is, today is a new day and you can make new choices that can give you a prosperous tomorrow.

So often I hear people say they want to exercise more and

eat healthier in order to get in better shape—but they never do. Some will start and stop after a week. Whether the reason to quit stems from a lack of interest or laziness, results will only happen if we remain consistent. If you can develop an unstoppable routine and stick to it, you will watch your life transform before your eyes. I don't know what you want out of life, but I do know that you must want it bad enough to give up temporary pleasure in exchange for your greatness. **Nothing changes by wishing, but everything changes with action.** If you don't like where you are right now, you owe it to yourself to do something about it.

Life is a process. You cannot become all you aspire to be in a day. Success takes time, so don't beat yourself up while in process. There's no such thing as an overnight success. David appeared to be an overnight success after he killed Goliath (1 Samuel 17:50). However, before the fight, he recounted that he was prepared because he had already killed a bear and a lion with his bare hands.

Preparation will always precede success. It is often said, and certainly true, that people are celebrated in public for what they practice in private. You may not be where you want to be, but you can begin to practice for where you are going. The future belongs to those who prepare for it. What are you trying to achieve in life? Look for someone who has done it successfully and model your approach after them. If someone else has done it, then you can do it.

Victoria Osteen recently posted a quote on social media that resonated with me saying, "Look for people that are doing what you want to do and be around them as much as you can because more is caught than taught." I don't know of any great person who didn't have someone or a group of people they looked up to.

Look for people you can learn from. There are unlimited amounts of useful resources online. Sift through them, find the ones that are valuable and apply them. Attend events, workshops, seminars, and conferences around you. Become intentional about your dreams and seize every opportunity in sight. Don't wait for the perfect moment to start your journey to greatness. There will never be a perfect time—so why wait? Act today, act now! Tomorrow is not guaranteed, the only time you have is now. We must answer Rabbi Hillel's question, "If not us, who? And if not now, when?" You are worthy of your dreams. If your dreams weren't possible, you wouldn't be holding them within you.

So often, I hear people say they are waiting for the "right time" to work on their dreams. Although I am completely in favor of waiting intentionally for something you desire, I also have a strong belief that waiting should not be passive. **Waiting doesn't equate idleness. Waiting is synonymous with preparation.** So, if you are in your waiting period, you've got to learn to wait actively. Athletes will tell you that when they train, their coaches will have them practice something called "active rest" between exercises. Active rest means instead of sitting on a bench to rest, you are instructed to jog in place or hold a plank position. While this may sound like torture to some, active rest actually makes the most of one's workout and ultimately increases efficiency. Active rest prepares you for the next move.

The concept of active rest can also be applied to our lives as we wait for the next opportunity to come. Rest is good, but too much rest can rob us of our next assignment. If we get too comfortable with our laurels, we begin to lose ground and it can become difficult to get back on track. Commit to actively waiting on your next assignment.

You've rested enough. It's time for you to get back in the game. You've doubted yourself enough. It's time to trust yourself like you never have before. Don't worry about how crazy your idea sounds. God has placed something in you that no one can take away. You weren't born to conform to this world, you were created to transform the world by the renewing of your mind (Romans 12:2).

Dean Alfange, an eminent American politician, once wrote a profound piece on the ideas of self-reliance and freedom titled, An American Creed. I pray the words will strike a chord in you as you read them here today:

I do not choose to be a common man,
It is my right to be uncommon... if I can,
I seek opportunity... not security.
I do not wish to be a kept citizen.
Humbled and dulled by having the
State look after me.
I want to take the calculated risk;
To dream and to build.
To fail and to succeed.
I refuse to barter incentive for a dole;
I prefer the challenges of life
To the guaranteed existence;

The thrill of fulfillment
To the stale calm of Utopia.
I will not trade freedom for beneficence
Nor my dignity for a handout
I will never cower before any master
Nor bend to any threat.
It is my heritage to stand erect.
Proud and unafraid;
To think and act for myself,
To enjoy the benefit of my creations
And to face the world boldly and say:
This, with God's help, I have done
All this is what it means
To be an American.

This quote was a game changer for me. It made me realize that I could simply be myself. I don't have to speak in a certain way or have a certain name to reach my goals. I have exactly what I need to make my goals and dreams happen, and so do you. Don't wish you were someone else and don't try to be like anyone else. We live in a world full of "wannabes" and people who aspire to be someone else. I don't know about you, but I refuse to be a "wannabe" and I challenge you to make that declaration too.

I believe I possess something powerful that the world has yet to see. I believe I'm significant. I believe I have the power to walk in my purpose. I encourage you to speak these words over yourself until you begin to believe them. Receive the courage to accept who you are. There are far too many counterfeits out there—I urge you not to add to the number.

Dare to be you! You are unstoppable when you are authentic and true.

5
YOU'VE GOT TO BE RELENTLESS

After my divorce, I felt as if my life had come to a complete stop. I was breathing, but not living on purpose. I was barely getting by each day. There was no passion in my daily life and I was not pursuing my dreams like I used to. I had acquired so much baggage from dwelling on the wrong that had been done to me that I spent my time rehearsing, recounting, and recanting the unfair treatment I had received. The pain was unbearable, and I wanted justice at all costs.

My desperation for justice began to overtake my thoughts and when justice didn't happen immediately, I was overtaken with frustration and angst. These negative feelings lingered for months and I fought to get my joy back. As I struggled, I realized the pain of recovery is much greater than the pain of injury.

When you are broken, God will often break you even further in order to make you whole again. The Bible says, "Yet you Lord, are our Father. We are the clay, you are the potter; we are all the work of your hand" (Isaiah 64:8 NIV). When a pot of clay is cracked, the potter fixes the crack by breaking the pot, watering the clay, and remolding the pot back together again. That's the process! That's what healing looks like. When the potter is done fixing the pot, it ends up looking better than it did before the crack.

That's exactly how God restores us. Restoration can be

painful, and it takes time to heal. So often, we just want to slap a piece of duct tape over what is hurting us and move on, but a broken heart cannot heal that way. Bishop TD Jakes once said, "There's no pill that can fix a broken heart." Only the love of our Father can heal something so tender and intimately deep. We must come to the point where we acknowledge that we cannot fix ourselves. Healing takes place when divinity meets humanity.

On a certain day, I came to myself, just as the prodigal son had in the famously told biblical parable in (Luke 5:17). I was tired of living in the past and wishing that things had turned out differently. At that moment, I was reminded that I have a higher calling upon my life and one bad experience was not going to rob me of my destiny.

A bad experience does not define who we are. Experiences, whether good or bad, are inevitable so long as we are alive. However, our perception of the experiences we've had will determine the way we live our lives. When we go through a traumatic experience, there is a tendency to assume life will always bring us pain—but nothing in life is permanent. Life is like the seasons; no one season lasts for forever. After every storm, there is sunshine; and there is always light at the end of the tunnel. That's just the structure of life, and you and I can do nothing about it. Now, we don't have to like the way life is set up, but we must understand the framework if we are going to be victorious in life.

Understanding the way life is structured helps us to better understand and accept our experiences. Rather than staying angry or frustrated with an unpleasant situation, choose to be happy and encouraged, knowing that no condition is permanent. It cannot rain on your parade forever. Someday the sun will shine on you. Be reminded that every storm will pass away, just as the seasons come and go.

When I decided to move past the pain and hurt from my losses, I had to start making healthy choices again. I began taking care of my spiritual, physical, mental, emotional, and financial health. I would pray, exercise, meditate and study because I desired change. Unpleasant experiences can cause us to become inactive, and inactivity is often accompanied by low self-esteem. If you are not in what you consider to be a healthier weight or appearance, you could be battling with low self-esteem issues. I am the happiest when I feel healthy and energetic—which is why I love to exercise. When I do so, I stimulate my brain cells and I get fired up about my goals. It's an avenue for me to release stress and maintain a positive outlook on life.

Prior to this time, every time I told my story, I told it to prove a point. I made sure my listeners understood that what I went through was not my fault but that of the other party. The problem with that was, my story was not empowering anybody. My perception was contrary to God's intent for my life. I realized God had given me a unique experience to empower the people I have been called to reach. I began to see how my experiences were tied to my destiny. I became more aware of the happenings around me and how they were shaping my life. I became very selective about the places I went and the people I associated with.

One day, I was in church and just before the service

began, I saw an announcement about Divorce Care on the screen. Immediately, I wrote down the information and went on to sign up to attend the class. Divorce Care is a program designed to help individuals who are either divorced or going through a divorce or separation. The class lasted for thirteen straight weeks. The timing wasn't convenient, but I committed to the schedule. I was in the right class with the right people for the right reason. I say everything was "right" not because I had all the time in the world to attend the class, but because I was determined to get the most out of the class.

In that class, I reconnected with Danielle, a friend I had worked with at a previous job. We were excited to meet again at a time when we needed each other the most. We partnered with Monica, another lady in the class, and our friendship took off from there. We were all at different stages in our divorce process, but we had one thing in common: our love for God. We trusted God and He brought us through the pain of divorce.

There will never be a perfect time to start working on yourself. The perfect time you have been waiting on is here. It's now. Fast forward to today, and Danielle is happily married to a wonderful man of God. She has also stepped into her calling. She is speaking at conferences, writing prayer books, and offering consulting services. God is doing mighty things through her and I am so proud of her. Monica is enjoying God's provision with her family and she is in a much better place. She's dating a godly man and she is very happy.

I share these personal stories of victory from my friends because there will always be a temptation to dwell on what didn't work, rather than focusing on the possibilities of what could happen. Remember, life is like the seasons and your struggles won't last forever. So, whatever you are going through, it must surely come to an end (Proverbs 23:18). Weeping may endure for a night, but joy comes in the morning (Psalms 30:5). If only you can endure the pain of your adversity for a time, you will soon rejoice with a crown on your head.

Nothing great happens without a fight. Challenges stretch us beyond our limits. They will test our faith and stretch our creative abilities if we let them. There's nothing you've been through that's new under the sun. Life happens to everyone. Have you ever gone through something that you thought would have taken you out, but somehow, you got through it and came out on the other side? I bet you have. That is proof that there is something greater in you that can withstand whatever life throws at you.

I was born and raised in Nigeria and destiny brought me to the United States in 2009. It would have been easier for me to settle for safe (after all, I was an alien in a foreign country). But I wanted God's best for my life, so I pursued my dreams even when it was hard. Life is hard. Life is not all about sunshine and rainbows. In one of her interviews, Christine Caine said that the most valuable advice she's ever given to her children is this: "Life is hard. Suck it up." In my opinion, there isn't a better way to sum it up. It simply is what it is. Life is beautiful, yet brutal.

It reminds me of Rocky Balboa's famous line in Rocky: "This thing called life will knock you down to your knees and keep you there permanently if you let it." Les Brown also has an antidote for when life knocks you down. He says, "When life knocks you down, try to land on your back because if you can look up, you can get up." Away with this fragile mentality we see in the world today—we've got to teach this generation what life is all about. **Without a strong sense of purpose, we will give up on life.** Nothing else hits us as hard as life will, but we've got to decide to stand back up after the hit. Your body can be wounded, but your spirit cannot be destroyed. You've got to resolve to rise above life's challenges. That's how you take dominion.

I have come to realize that if we do what is easy, life will be hard for us; but if we do what is hard, life will be easy. This sounds like a paradox, doesn't it? Well, life is paradoxical. To live a life of dominion, you've got be willing to be uncomfortable and unreasonable. Nothing great happens within your comfort zone, so step out of it. Step into a higher zone where you have no limitations with endless opportunities. In this zone, you determine how much you get out of life. Dare to take steps, even when you cannot see the staircase. That's faith!

The Bible says to walk by faith, not by sight (2 Corinthians 5:7). The night I decided to leave the abusive marriage I was in, I had no clue where I was going, but I stepped out anyway. Women often remain in abusive relationships much longer than they should because they fear what their lives will become without the relationship. But, they should be more fearful of what their lives may become if they remain abused.

Your life is far too precious for anyone to toil with. You've got to understand that the very nature of your destiny is independent of anything else. Your destiny is not dependent on a person, a place, or a thing. The people we trust may disappoint us, but God never fails. No one is your source but God. You may have walked into an abusive relationship by accident, but you do not have to remain there for the rest of your life. Remaining in an abusive marriage is like laying down your life for the abuser and thinking your blood can save the marriage. But only the Blood of Jesus can save and deliver. Quit acting like you have the power to change another person. The only person you can change is you.

Make yourself a priority in your own life. No one will love you more than you love yourself. Are you catching it yet? The only common denominator here is you. You determine what happens to you, no one else does. The power to call the shots in your life was placed inside of you before the foundations of the world were formed. No man born of a woman can take that away from you.

After I left my abuser, he came after me and collected all he had purchased for me. His intent was to ground me so I would return to him, but I refused to return to captivity. I was committed to living free or dying in the process. Remember: no one leaves this life alive so, what are you afraid of?

DISCOVER WHO YOU ARE

If you don't discover who you are and what you possess, people will try to offer you what is already yours just to make themselves feel important. I am here to tell you that no one can give you what you already have, and no one can make you who you already are. The last I checked, you were made in the image and the likeness of God. You have the mind of Christ, so you can be like Him, talk like Him, and live like Him.

All that you will ever need is already inside of you. You have all it takes to live a life of purpose and contribution. When God created you, He created His kind. You are the express image of your Father. You have His DNA running through your veins. You are more powerful than you can ever begin to image. You have a godly heritage. In your Father's house, there are many rooms (John 14:1-3). It is your birthright to stand up unafraid because your Father in Heaven owns the universe.

Sadly, if you are unaware of who you are, you will live below your potential. You are royalty—don't live like a peasant. It's critical that we increase our level of consciousness on a daily basis so we don't lose sight of who we are. It's one thing to be born great, but it's another thing to believe you are great. Faith is your belief in motion. The Bible says that if we believe, then we will receive whatever we ask for in prayer (Matthew 21:22). In other words, if you believe, you can become anything you want to become.

No wonder Carter G. Woodson said, "If you can control a man's thinking you do not have to worry about his action. When you determine what a man shall think you do not have to concern yourself about what he will do. If you make a man feel that he is inferior, you do not have to compel him to accept an inferior status, for he will seek it himself. If you make a man think that he is justly an outcast, you do not have to order him to the back door. He will go without being told;

and if there is no back door, his very nature will demand one."

Whatever you believe you are, is exactly who you will become. Faith is hearing on replay. Your thinking is constantly expanding by the words you hear. Faith is a catalyst that swings you into action. The more you hear, the more likely you are to act with certainty. My brother has been very instrumental in my growth in this area. Years ago, I had tried to start a business that failed; leaving me in a desperate financial situation. My brother gave me some audio books by Jim Rohn, Les Brown, Ron Carpenter, Joel Osteen, Grant Cardone, and Tony Robbins. These men are respected authorities in their various areas of expertise and their teachings revolutionized my thinking. I listened to these men until their philosophies were engraved in my mind. The more I listened to them, the more confident I became. I felt empowered to get back into the game of life and win, all because I realized that I alone had the power to set myself up to succeed.

Do you know you can set the tone for each day just by cranking up your faith early in the morning? I often hear people say, "I need a cup of coffee to start my day." But those people don't realize that there is something much stronger than the kick from a cup of coffee. The words you choose to hear when the day breaks are a significant tool for your success.

When I learned the power of my own words over my thoughts, I began to wake up each morning declaring:

"This is the day that the Lord has made, and I will rejoice and

be glad in it. I can do all things through Christ who strengthens me. I have the power to create wealth. God has given me special gifts and I am going to share them with others. I have dominion over every situation in my life. I am a territorial commander. I have the anointing to break yokes. I am armed and dangerous. I crush goals and I slay giants. I am indestructible. I have the life of Christ in me, therefore, I can think like Christ, speak like Christ, and live like Christ. I am unstoppable."

This type of declaration is unconventional, but it works. You have the power to declare what kind of day you want to have. We've got to approach each day with a winning mentality.

Your attitude will determine your outcome at the end of each day. I remember sitting for a board exam, and I was nervous while preparing for it. I decided I was going to shake off the anxiety by declaring my success in advance. Each time I felt nervous about the exam, I declared the following words aloud:

"I have the mental ability to pass this exam. I have the critical thinking skills required for success. I demand my subconscious mind to bring forth the knowledge I have deposited. I have never failed an exam in my life and this exam will not be an exception."

I wrote these words in my journal and I recited them several times a day. When you have prepared thoroughly for a task and you still feel jitters, declare your success aloud and it will become reality. On the day of the exam, I woke up with unbelievable confidence and I attacked the exam with certainty. Not only did I pass the exam, but I realized I could do anything I can make myself believe. After this discovery, I became very aware of the power that lies within me—and that same power lies in everyone who believes. You simply have to call it forth.

Jim Rohn put it so well when he said, "Everything we want is within reach." The big question is this: How many people are going to reach? The apple does not fall far from the tree. Success does leave clues. If you search for the clues, you will find them. You may not have what you need, but if you search for it, you are guaranteed to find it. The Bible says, "Ask and it shall be given, seek and you shall find, knock and it shall be opened" (Matthew 7:7 KJV). Dare to ask for what you want. Ask intelligently, ask specifically, and ask believing you will receive. You wouldn't have the dreams you are having if you weren't capable of achieving them. You have the power to make your dreams come true.

Tony Robbins helped me understand the power of incantation. Incantation is simply saying something you believe with power and certainty. This is a powerful spiritual exercise that can build one's faith when done repeatedly with understanding. Tony Robbins is a great advocate for incantation and he attributes his massive success to this spiritual exercise. Since he was 17, every time before he goes out to speak he will say the follow words repeatedly: "I now command my subconscious mind to direct me in helping as many people as possible today to better their lives, by giving me the strength, the emotion, the persuasion, the humor, the brevity, whatever it takes to show these people and get these people to change their lives now!"

This is the kind of certainty that we need to have about our dreams and what we have been called to do. If no one can talk you out of what you know you were born to do, then you are certainly on your way to success. If you are uncertain about your life, you can begin practicing this exercise too. People who are certain are not more powerful than others—they simply know how to use the power that lies within them. Quit feeling intimidated when you meet people who are more confident than you are. Instead, let their confidence inspire you to reach higher. Dare to train your mind to believe in the power that lies within you.

The Bible says, "You will also declare a thing, and it will be established for you; so light will shine on your ways" in Job 22:28 (NKJV). This is why it is important that we say the things we want and not the things we don't want. If you say something long enough, you will have it. When I was married to my now ex-husband, each time we had an argument he threatened that he was going to get a divorce. Well, sure enough, within two years of saying those words repeatedly, he got exactly what he asked for.

You will reap what you sow and being unaware of this principle does not exempt you from it. Our words are powerful, and we need to speak words that work for us, not against us. Proverbs 18:21 (NKJV) declares, "Death and life are in the power of the tongue." You've got to become aware of what you hear and what you see because these things will inevitably create the thoughts you have, and you will naturally move in the direction of your thoughts. You cannot afford to be a casual thinker. We can challenge our mentality by searching for good information. This is the beginning of personal development.

In the world we live in today, we have more access to information than ever before. However, information by itself has no power until it is applied. Given the proliferation of information, it is important that we are selective about what we choose to ingest. Not every piece of information out there is wholesome, so it is our responsibility to choose wisely. The information you don't apply will not change your life. Though this sounds like common knowledge, it is not common practice. I know of people who shop for workout gear and equipment that they will never use. It's no wonder why they are overweight and unhappy. In other words, it is not enough to know something. Until you apply what you know, your life remains the same and the struggle continues. This fact only reinforces that we determine the outcome of our lives. We have the power to decide which way we want to go in life. You can start practicing today for where you want to be tomorrow.

When I decided to commit to writing this book, I practiced writing a paragraph every day. I figured, if I stuck to the plan, I would be finished within a year. I realized that if you simplify a task, it becomes easier to achieve. Think about your dreams and simplify them into small tasks you can accomplish every day. If you commit to doing the little tasks daily and consistently, you will accomplish a lot with ease. So often, we try to figure out the complexities of a project before we even start, and that discourages us from doing anything because it overwhelms us. But remember the age-old phrase, "Rome was not built in a day." Focus on laying one block at a time, and soon you will have a wall. It will take a while to accomplish your dreams, but simple consistent steps will surely get you there.

Some people are very good at starting out strong, but they never finish because they lack discipline. Make discipline a major force in your life. Les Brown says, "To be successful, you must be willing to do the things today others won't do in order to have the things tomorrow others won't have." Those who have made discipline a priority in their lives will lead over those who haven't. Think about it like this: those who work out consistently are those who get paid to train those who don't. So, failing to become disciplined is relegating yourself to a position where you are led by those who are.

Discipline is hard, but so is life. I have realized that there are two types of pain in life and each of us will undeniably experience one of the two: the pain of discipline and the pain of regret. The first weighs in ounces while the latter weighs in tons. The pain of discipline is temporary, but the pain of regret could last a lifetime. Regret stems from the things we should have done but failed to do. I have chosen the pain of discipline, and I urge you to do the same.

Your emotions will never cooperate with your goals. Athletes don't wake up every morning feeling like going to practice, but they condition their minds and get their bodies moving. That is discipline! I love what Augusta Kantra said about discipline: "Discipline is choosing between what you want now and what you want the most." I hear a lot of people say, "I don't feel like it today," but guess what? No one ever feels like it all the time. Discipline is what makes you pursue your goals even when you don't feel like it. You cannot let your emotions dictate what you do. You've got to learn to tame your feelings, so they do not stop you from becoming who you were created to be.

Begin to structure your life for success today. No one ever stumbles upon success. The path to success is traveled by those who are intentional about the actions they take. The daily rituals you have will determine the course of your life and where you end up. Many of us know the things we should be doing or could be doing, but we do not do them. It's time to turn your "should" into a "must." You cannot wish for things to happen—you've got to make them happen.

Put a stake in the ground and commit to your life. Quit procrastinating and get to work. We often say things like, "When I get married," or "When I get the job," or "When I start the business," then we will do this and that—but we never do. We push things away and give reasons to justify why we can't do them right now. The big question is this: How much time do you think you have? No one knows. So, why live your life procrastinating as if you have a thousand years to live? Believe it or not, our days are numbered, so we must live purposefully. Yesterday is gone, tomorrow is not guaranteed, and the only time we have is now. Live in the moment and give your dreams all you've got. In the words of my brother, I say to you: "Live life at full crush."

HOW LOW CAN YOU GO?

Trees grow from the ground up. Buildings are built from ground zero. Everything in life begins from scratch. The way to the top is at the bottom. The bottom is where the magic happens. Everyone at the peak of their career will tell you they once started at the bottom of the ladder. No one starts off at the top. You serve your way up from the bottom. Greatness lies in your service. Bishop T.D. Jakes puts it this way when he says, "Greatness is not determined by how high you can go, but how low you can go." So, the question becomes: How low can you go?

The lower you go, the greater you become. The Bible says, "The greatest among you will be your servant" in Matthew 23:11 (NIV). In other words, leaders are servants. Your desire to lead is determined by your ability to serve. My local pastor, Stephen Hayes, shared an anonymous quote about service in one of his recent sermons saying, "If serving is below you then leadership is beyond you." Service is the key that unlocks the door of opportunity.

Think about the famous story of David and Goliath found in (1 Samuel 17: 1-58) for a moment. We tend to focus on David's victory over Goliath, but David wouldn't have had the opportunity to fight against Goliath had he not been willing to serve. David was asked by his father to take food to his brothers on the battlefield. David didn't have to serve his brothers. After all, they never acknowledged him, so he had reasons not to be kind to them. But he knew better. He understood the value of service. David was not part of the Israeli army, but his willingness to serve those on the army line (his brothers) gave him the opportunity to be at the battlefield.

If you serve others, you will have access to areas where

you would not have access otherwise. If you help enough people get what they want, you will have all that you want and more. Your success is tied to your service. Never pass up on an opportunity to serve. And most importantly, serve with joy. Zig Ziglar said, "Your attitude, not your aptitude, will determine your altitude." No one can ever rise above the attitude they have toward the people they serve. Not everyone will appreciate your service—but remember, your service is not unto man but God.

God is the one who rewards a diligent servant. Robert Greene, author of the best-selling book, *The 48 Laws of Power*, shared some unequivocal truths about power. The first law in his book states: "Never outshine thy master." He urges us to always make our masters (the people we serve) more powerful than they appear. Sometimes we find ourselves under the authority of a leader that is less talented than we expected them to be, and we could be tempted to disregard their authority. There is also the temptation to go against a master's directive if it's not in line with ours. But these temptations can be costly if we act on them.

There's a story from the Bible that tells us of a servant named Gehazi who paid dearly for despising his master's order. In 2 Kings Chapter 5, there was a wealthy, famous soldier named Naaman who suffered from leprosy. The prophet Elisha instructed him to bathe in the Jordan River and he was healed. Naaman returned to Elisha with a gift, however, Elisha refused the gift and his servant, Gehazi, was not pleased with that. Gehazi went after Naaman and took from him what his master had refused. Gehazi's greed and

TAKE DOMINION

disregard for his master's order led to his master cursing him and his descendants with leprosy.

This story is quite scary, but it does sound a note of warning to all who serve. We all have people in our lives that we serve with our time, our energy, and our resources—so we need to ensure that our service is mixed with love. That's how we will receive favor in the sight of God and man. In a world where the majority of people are asking what others can do for them, ask what you can do for others. Remember: you were made to serve, not to be served.

SEPARATION IS PART OF THE DEAL

When God wants to do something spectacular in you and through you, He separates you from the crowd. When God calls you, He sets you apart from the familiar. You may even feel deserted, as some people will walk away from you—not because they don't like you, but because they can't understand the move of God in your life.

The more room you create for God in your life, the less room there would be for other things. **More of God means less of you—and less of everyone and everything else.** You ought to get comfortable with people leaving you. Not everyone is called to be in your life forever. It's often said that some people are in your life for a season, others for a reason, and only a handful for a lifetime. The understanding of the different categories of people we encounter in life can save us from feeling resentful when people walk away or quit being loyal to us.

Separation is inevitable when God is at work in your life.

- 96 -

He does it for a couple of reasons, one of which being: God wants us to put our trust in Him, and Him alone. This is what the Lord says in Jeremiah 17:5 (NIV): "Cursed is the one who trusts in man, who draws strength from mere flesh and whose heart turns away from the Lord." No doubt God uses people to bless us; however, they are not our source—God is.

When we seek God first, we will gain everything else we hope for (Matthew 6:33-34). When we pursue God, not only does He reveal our purpose to us, He begins to shape our character, so we can attract purposeful relationships. About three years after my divorce, I thought I was ready to date, so I was expecting to be approached by men. But that never happened. I questioned myself, wondering if I was even attractive. As I began to seek the face of God regarding my desires to be married again, God began to reveal to me what His intentions were. He was separating me from the pursuit of men on purpose. He wanted me to heal from the hurt I had experienced in my previous marriage. He wanted me to become whole again. I began to realize that I didn't need a man to complete me and that I was complete in Christ.

No man or woman can make you feel whole. It's not the responsibility of anyone to make you feel complete. It is our responsibility to search within ourselves to see where we've been broken and invite God to heal us. It takes a lot of courage to come face to face with our brokenness because it is often easier to conceal a defect.

Earlier, I told you I had Chickenpox while carrying my second child and it left a scar around my neckline. I do everything possible to conceal the scar, and many of us do the same with our brokenness. We tend to cover up our brokenness like scars, thereby increasing our level of insecurity without even knowing it. God wants to heal our scars and our brokenness. However, He is waiting for us to reveal them to Him. God will not heal what you don't admit you have. I have learned to surrender to the Lord over and over so that He can perfect His will in my life. Today, I'm a wife to the most amazing husband on the planet, and I'm so glad I yielded to God's calling upon my life. Whenever you feel deserted and alone, it may be an indication that you have something concealed that needs to be revealed. Remember: we serve a faithful God who loves us regardless of our scars and brokenness.

6
THE MANIFESTATION

There's nothing more compelling than a man or woman whose time has come. No devil in hell, no man born of a woman, no principality or power can withstand a person whose time has come. When the time comes for a child to crawl, walk, or talk—nothing stops them; they simply do so. Time makes these stages of child development possible without any special procedures. This goes to show that there is time for everything.

Time is required for your dreams to come to reality. Time is required for the healing of your heart. Time is required for change to become significant. Everything in life is a process and process requires time. You cannot conceive an idea today and birth it tomorrow. You've got to go through the process of developing that idea to maturity.

Each one of us can be likened to a seed. When a seed is planted, watered, and nourished—it flourishes. But seeds are small and until they are planted, they cannot grow. This analogy reminds me of myself, and I hope you can relate. Planting a seed literally means burying the seed in the ground and covering it in dirt. When I was in seed form, I felt very small and insignificant. I knew the potential of the seed within me, but in faith, I submitted myself to being planted. Sometimes we think the planting of our seed means covering our potential, but planting only means protecting the tenderness of what we carry.

What you carry within you—no matter how potent— must be developed. If your seed is going to have root and eventually become a tree, then it must be planted in dirt. Being planted in dirt can look like isolation or rejection. You could feel discouraged and you may be overlooked—but these things do not negate the fact that you are a tree in the making. You are gradually becoming who you were created to be.

Don't get confused when you meet people at a lofty stage in their lives and assume they have always been this way. Everyone goes through a process of growth and it's okay to embrace where you are in the process. You don't have to feel so intimidated by someone else's growth that you begin to uproot your own seed. Trust the process you are in and stay focused. Growth is an undertaking that requires time. Growth entails pruning, cutting, and trimming—all of which are painful.

What if I told you that your pleasure will come from your pain? No one will birth their dream without tears. Pain is not enjoyable, but it is part of the process. Your endurance must be tested. Your faith must be tried. Paul says, in James 1:2-3 (NIV), "Consider it pure joy, my brothers and sisters, whenever you face trials of many kinds, because you know that the testing of your faith produces perseverance." Perseverance is built over time. Understanding time and process eliminates worry, anxiety, and frustration from our lives. Be patient with yourself, knowing you are growing every day. Think of your life as a time-release capsule that releases in part at a specific time.

I love the scripture that says, "I returned, and saw under the sun, that the race is not to the swift, nor the battle to the strong, neither yet bread to the wise, nor yet riches to men of understanding, nor yet favor to men of skill; but time and chance happens to them all" (Ecclesiastes 9:11 KJV). Time and opportunity determine growth, strength, and riches. What we do with our time and the opportunities we have will determine what we get out of life. This means everyone has an equal chance to win because we determine what we do with our time and the opportunities we have. Don't let another opportunity pass you by. Your time is here. Your time is now. Remember you are unstoppable!

USE WHAT YOU HAVE

Have you ever asked yourself the question, "How in the world did I make it through that?" The answer is simple: You are made of so much more than you could ever begin to imagine. But you will never know what you are made of until you encounter defeat, failure, loss, or pain.

I wouldn't have known what I now know about myself had I not experienced defeat, failure, loss, and pain along the way. I thought I was going to lose my mind when I was going through the worst times of my life, but that was when I realized I was greater than anything that ever confronted me. I never knew I could survive the loss of my father and brother. I never knew I could recover from a failed marriage. You will never know what you can rise from until you fall. I discovered my purpose right in the middle of my pain. The idea to write this book came to me the same year I was going through a divorce. **You can make the most challenging time of your life the most rewarding if you decide to.** I have learned to see the good in every situation.

So often, we beat ourselves up for the mistakes we've made, and if we are not careful, we begin to condemn ourselves. No matter how badly you think you've messed up, Jesus still loves you. The Bible says in Romans 5:8 (NIV), "But God demonstrates his love for us in this: While we were still sinners, Christ died for us." The love of Christ is unconditional. It's okay to acknowledge your mistakes, but you don't have to dwell on them. You can assume responsibility for your life without self-condemnation.

Romans 8:1 (NKJV) says, "There is therefore now no condemnation to those who are in Christ Jesus, who do not walk according to the flesh, but according to the Spirit." We cannot continue to condemn ourselves for the things God has already redeemed us from. Don't let the mistakes of the past keep you bound with guilt and shame. Once you confess your sins, let them go and decide not to go back to them. The grace of God is available to all of us, but we've got to be willing to receive it and live freely.

Receiving the grace of God activates the power within us to change the situation around us. You have so much potential on the inside of you, and only challenges can bring out the more in you. Life is full of difficulties that will either break you or make you. I have realized that some people get lost in the fire while others are built from it. I believe you are one of those who will be built from the fire. **The pressure of life is real, but even more real is the power that lies within you.**

The fight is on, so I urge you to put on the whole armor of God that you may be able to stand against the wiles of the devil (Ephesians 6:11-18). To have victory over the challenges of life, you will first need to wear the belt of truth to come to terms with reality. Accept that you have been broken, and receive the grace of God that can heal your brokenness.

Second, you need to put on the breastplate of righteousness to be a lover of good and not evil. Restrain from anything that does not bring glory to God. Commit to living a life of integrity and excellence.

Third, wear the shoes of peace that come from the gospel and avoid strife at all costs. Learn to live peaceably with all men. Meditate on the word of God, day and night. Let the Word of God be engraved in your heart, and let your life mirror that of Christ.

Fourth, take the shield of faith so you can quench the fiery darts of the evil one and believe what the Word of God says about you. You don't have to see to believe. Faith is believing regardless of what you are seeing right now. Call forth the things that are not as though they are. Learn to see beyond your eyesight.

Fifth, put the helmet of salvation and carry the sword of the spirit, which is the Word of God. You cannot win the battle you are in by your own strength. There is a higher power, a higher name that can save and deliver. His name is Jesus. There is no one greater than Him. In Him, there is life everlasting.

Finally, pray at all times. Let God be the center of everything you do. Speak to Him before you take any step concerning your life. Don't withhold any part of yourself from Him. Let Him have it all. You are better off when He is in control of your life. Don't let life beat you down again before you surrender to Him. He is the way—the only way—the truth, and the life (John 14:6).

You may get discouraged when you look at what you have in comparison to what you want to accomplish. You may think you have less than you need but in reality, you have more than enough. What you have will only multiply when you begin to use it. How is it that Jesus fed five thousand people with what seemed to be insufficient? His disciples thought what they had was not enough to feed the crowd, and rightly so. But after Jesus blessed and broke the bread, it began to multiply. Your miracle happens when you begin to use what you have. At that moment, you will realize you have more than enough. The disciples gathered twelve baskets of leftovers after feeding the crowd. But, they wouldn't have realized they had more than enough if they had not attempted to feed the crowd with what they had (Matthew 14:13-21, Mark 6:31-44, Luke 9:12-17, John 6:1-14).

Most times we are stuck because we fail to use what we have, wishing we had more to work with. In 1 Kings 17:7-16 the prophet Elijah was talking to the widow of Zarephath. Elijah asked the widow to give him a cup of water and a piece of bread.

So, she said, "As the Lord your God lives, I do not have bread, only a handful of flour in a bin, and a little oil in a jar; and see, I am gathering a couple of sticks that I may go in and prepare it for myself and my son, that we may eat it, and die."

And Elijah said to her, "Do not fear; go and do as you have

said, but make me a small cake from it first, and bring it to me; and afterward make some for yourself and your son. For thus says the Lord God of Israel: 'The bin of flour shall not be used up, nor shall the jar of oil run dry, until the day the Lord sends rain on the earth'" (1 Kings 17:13-14 NKJV).

"So, she went away and did according to the word of Elijah; and she and he and her household ate for many days. The bin of flour was not used up, nor did the jar of oil run dry, according to the word of the Lord which He spoke by Elijah" (1 Kings 17:16 NKJV).

God will multiply what you have once you put it to use. The widow in this story didn't have enough at the time Elijah asked her to make bread for him, but as soon as she began to make the bread, the flour and oil never ran out.

Your gift will not look sufficient until you begin to use it. You may think you don't have a story big enough to make a book, but you can start journaling. Your ideas will expand once you begin to write. The miracle happens when you step out in faith with what you have. Put what you have to work, and you will be amazed at the multiplication that will follow. What you have in your hand is more than enough.

When God told Moses to appear before Pharaoh in Exodus 3:10 and demand that the children of Israel be released, he was beyond nervous. Moses was afraid that the people would not believe that God had sent him.

Then the Lord said to him, "What is that in your hand?"

"A staff," he replied.

The Lord said, "Throw it on the ground."

Moses threw it on the ground and it became a snake, and

he ran from it. Then the Lord said to him, "Reach out your hand and take it by the tail." So Moses reached out and took hold of the snake and it turned back into a staff in his hand… so that they may believe that the Lord, the God of their fathers, the God of Abraham, the God of Isaac, and the God of Jacob, has appeared to you" (Exodus 4:2-5 NIV).

Most of us are just like Moses in this way: we have a rod in our hands, but we don't realize the rod is not ordinary. What you have may not be fancy in your eyes, but you will never know the potential until you begin to work it. The rod in your hand is more than just a rod—it will become whatever it needs to be once you cast it to the ground. So often we desire to have the rod in other people's hands because it looks better than ours. But what we fail to realize is that our rod can do the same, and even more, if we would just use it.

Moses never knew the rod in his hand could part the Red Sea until he stretched it over the water. God is waiting for you to use what He has given you. He will perform the miracle once you put your rod to use. Remember: what you have is more than enough.

WHAT DO YOU SEE?

What do you see when you look at your life? The way we perceive our lives is very critical to the outcome we experience.

In the first chapter of the book of Jeremiah, God asked Jeremiah, "What do you see?"

Jeremiah replied, "I see a branch of an almond tree."

Then the Lord said, "You have seen well; for I am ready to perform My Word" (Jeremiah 1:11 NKJV).

From this conversation, it's clear that Jeremiah could perceive something his physical eyes couldn't see. Perception goes beyond what your eyes can see. Perception is what your mind can see. Jeremiah could see through his mind's eye to what he wanted, and God essentially said to him, "Consider it done!"

We must learn to speak and declare the things we can only see through our mind's eye. That's faith! "Faith it" until it becomes reality. This is not to say you should be in denial of your current situation—but begin to see what is possible in your life. Sometimes we hold back on saying what we can perceive in our mind's eye because our present condition looks nothing like what we are desiring. Do not make the mistake of spending precious time trying to figure out how it will all work out. Trust that God, who has given you a mind to perceive the unseen, will make your dreams come to life.

Perception is a powerful tool of the mind that has creative abilities. It's almost impossible to perceive something and not act toward it. Remember faith without works is dead. When I began to imagine myself performing book signings and speaking at events, I knew I didn't have to wait for a publisher or promoter to endorse me. I began writing this book, even when I had no idea how it would be published or promoted.

That's an example of a practical walk of faith. Don't let your sight fool you. Allow your mind to capture what your eyes cannot. You cannot afford to see yourself just the way you are. There's more to you than your physical eyes can see. See yourself through the eyes of potential, and in the process of time, you will become more than you could have ever imagined.

Proverbs 23:7 (NKJV) says, "For as a man thinks in his heart, so is he." **If all you can see is what your eyes can behold then you cannot possess anything beyond your physical sight.** No one can ever rise above his or her perception. You cannot perceive yourself as cursed and be blessed. What you see is what you get. Use the power of perception to your advantage. Begin to see your life as blessed through your mind's eye. God is waiting for you to tell Him what you see about yourself. Do as Jeremiah did, and God will hasten to perform that which you have seen.

What dreams has God placed inside of your heart? Joseph, the son of Jacob, is another person we can reference on this subject. God gave Joseph a clear picture of his future through dreams. Even though his brothers were envious of him and thought of him as boastful, his dreams came to pass many years and many trials later (Genesis 37:5-8).

It doesn't matter how ridiculous or far-fetched your dreams may sound—they are possible if only you can believe. Nothing is impossible to those that believe (Mark 9:23). God is faithful, and He wouldn't show us a picture to tease us. He is a God of integrity. If He shows you a picture through your mind's eye, you can rest assured that He will hasten to perform it.

HE ALWAYS USES THE UNLIKELY

God will always use the unlikely to fulfill His purpose. If you have ever been overlooked, underestimated, or considered an underdog—then you are the most likely person to be chosen by God.

When God wanted to appoint a king in Israel from the house of Jesse, He chose the unlikely son of Jesse named David. When the prophet, Samuel, came to the house of Jesse to anoint the king, he was captivated by the outward appearance of the other sons, but God told Samuel he hadn't chosen any of them. Samuel said to Jesse, "Are all the young men here?"

Jesse responded, "There remains yet the youngest, and there he is, keeping the sheep" (1 Samuel 16:11 NKJV).

Notice that David was not even given a prior invitation to appear before Samuel because he was overlooked. However, the same one who was overlooked for being too young and too small was the very one God chose to anoint as king. Men will often size you up based on your outward appearance, but God looks at the heart (1 Samuel 16:7). The very thing men cannot see in you is what God will use to amaze them.

Shortly after my separation from my ex-husband, he thought I wouldn't be able to make it without him. His parents assured him that I was going to return. They all underestimated the power of God in me. They thought to themselves, "She has no family here, and surely she wouldn't survive without us. Let's see how she's going to raise two children by herself!"

Little did they know that God had chosen to crown me with His goodness and mercy. Who would have thought that a book would be the outcome of my worst experience? Who would have thought that my pain would give me such a strong sense of purpose? Who would have thought that the very stone the builders rejected would become the chief cornerstone?

Don't fret when men reject you—it simply means God approves of you. Don't try to fit into someone else's mold. You were made different for God's glory. Dare to be different even when you run the risk of being labeled as "the unlikely one." God is perfect in all His ways. He placed His power in the most unlikely place: right inside of you. Refuse to be ordinary—be mysterious! Let your ways remain a mystery to those who think they can predict your future. Only a person who lacks understanding will attempt to underestimate what you can do. Your abilities are immeasurable because of the power of God that lies within you.

When God created you, He placed everything you could ever need to live a purposeful life right inside of you. You are a spirit being with the mind of Christ. Romans 8:11 (NKJV) tells us that the "Spirit of Him who raised Jesus from the dead dwells in you." The Bible refers to the Holy Spirit as our advocate, sent by the Father to teach us all things and remind us of everything the Father has told us. You have a well of the Spirit of God in you, but it is your responsibility to draw from it.

The power of the Holy Spirit must be activated for it to become potent. The activation of the Spirit is what produces power. Now, this is not a one-time activation. It is a daily activation that produces a stronger and deeper relationship with our Father in heaven. Each day when you wake up, you must activate the power that lies within you. This is where you draw inspiration from. You cannot afford to wait for someone else to come along and inspire you. What if they never show up? You've got to be your own inspiration. You have all it takes to fulfill your dreams because of the Spirit of God in you.

In the beginning, it was recorded that the earth was without form and void—darkness covered the face of the earth. But then God said, "Let there be light," and there was light (Genesis 1:3 NKJV).

Your life may be without form right now. You could be in a dark season or there could be a void in your life, but I am here to tell you that the Spirit of God within you will hover over your life and create a new thing. You have the power to bind the things that you don't want by the Spirit, and in the same breath, you can loose the things you do want in your life. Remember it is all within you.

When I realized the potency of the power within me I began to create the life I wanted from within. What is on the inside will always outlast what is on the outside. We tend to nurture what is on the outside more than we do what is on the inside. This is not to say there is anything wrong with that, the only problem is everything on the outside will fade. As time goes by, we lose our vitality, our youth, the glow on our skin and so on. The one thing that is ever-living is the spirit within us because it is alive in Christ and Christ lives forever.

I would rather invest more of my time and energy into what I have within than what I have on the outside. The irony of what lies on the inside is that no one sees it and because we desire to be noticed, we focus far more on our outward appearance. When people look at you, they may comment on your outward appearance by saying things like, "You have thick eyebrows," or "You have beautiful eyes." But how many times has someone told you, "You have a powerful spirit inside of you," or commented on the state of your inner being? Rarely!

The point is that what is on the inside is rarely as popular as the exterior. Most people are going to judge you based solely on what they see outwardly, but that will never diminish the power you have on the inside. David did not look like he could slay a giant. The Bible tells us he was "but a youth, ruddy, and of a fair countenance" in 1 Samuel 17:42 (NKJV). However, David was very confident in who he was on the inside. He knew that the Spirit of God in Him could slay the giant before him.

Train for what you possess on the inside. Before David fought Goliath, he had been training in the fields with bears and lions. When the time came to fight against Goliath, he was fearless because he was prepared for the fight. Never go into a battle unprepared. Life is a battle. No wonder David praised God for training his hands to war and his fingers to fight (Psalms 144:1).

There is a constant battle between light and darkness, good and evil, right and wrong, life and death, health and sickness, wealth and poverty, success and failure, hard work and laziness, love and hate, strength and weakness—and the list can go on and on. But preparation for the battle always starts from within. You must be ready and able to win the battle before you can actually win.

Those who have beat cancer will tell you that their healing began from within, even when the test results proved otherwise. It doesn't matter what the facts are saying about you—your victory lies within. Your spirit is stronger than anything that is confronting you. Your Father in heaven is called the Lion of the tribe of Judah and He cannot be defeated. And guess what? He lives inside of you.

UNIQUE

You are unique. You are so unique that no one has, or will ever have, your exact fingerprint. You are so unique that no one can be you—even if they tried to be. This truth ought to make you love yourself. To know that no one on the face of the earth can be compared to you is the greatest feeling anyone can have. God made you different from everyone else for a reason. He wants you to not compare yourself to anyone else because you cannot be duplicated. You ought to feel confident when you are in the midst of people knowing that no one else has what you have. Everyone is unique and special in their own right.

What if you didn't have to compare yourself to anyone else? Imagine the pressure you could be taking off your shoulders. Quit comparing yourself to others so you can start developing yourself into God's masterpiece. There's nothing wrong with being inspired by someone else, but don't let that put a cap on your growth or turn you into a competitor. You were not born to compete, rather you were born to have dominion over all the resources your Father created.

Competitiveness is not a trait of a winner. When you are in competition with others, you are secretly wishing for them to fail so you can win. Competition will stunt your growth and make you a hater instead of a lover. On the other hand, confidence is a trait of a winner. Winners are never threatened by someone else's success. They celebrate others and are constantly working on themselves to become better.

Everyone was born to win. But while some are winning, others have yet to discover the winning life.

Proverbs 27:17 (NKJV) says, "As iron sharpens iron; so a man sharpens the countenance of his friend." We need relationships with others to make it in life. Inspiration is what makes us better than who we were yesterday. If we can remove the toxicity of comparison from our hearts and minds, then we will experience incredible growth in every area of our lives. You cannot be like anyone else, but you can be the best version of yourself.

I am nowhere close to the person I was in 2009 when I arrived in the United States. I have watched myself evolve throughout the years. I have fallen in love with me because I am the only one I can change. I have adjusted my mindset, time and time again, and my life has literally transformed as a result. I cannot be duplicated; therefore, I am irreplaceable. I am one of a kind and so are you. What is yours no one can take, so don't operate in fear. People can speak like you, walk like you and even act like you—but they can never be you. Therefore, be brave and approach life with confidence.

I no longer feel intimidated when I am around successful people because I have learned to draw inspiration from them. When you are open to ideas from other people, it keeps you from being critical. It is interesting to me how people can be critical of what others do simply because they are not the ones doing it. Don't waste time hating on someone else, simply because they are acting on the things you haven't had the courage to pursue. No one is stopping you from taking control over your life. There's nothing more frustrating than living beneath your purpose—the feeling of knowing there's something more within you, but still settling for less. It takes courage to assume the role you've been called to play in life.

After the death of Moses in Joshua 1:1-3, Joshua became the next leader of the people of Israel. God assured Joshua that He would be with him, just as He was with Moses. God made a special promise to Joshua when He said, "No one will be able to stand before you all the days of your life: as I was with Moses, so I will be with you: I will not leave you, nor forsake you" (Joshua 1:5 NIV). Just as God was counting on Joshua to lead His people, He is counting on you to fulfill His purpose for your life. He is letting you know that no one will be able to take on your assignment, even if they tried.

Destiny is personal. Your walk is different from my walk, so we are co-workers in our Father's vineyard. You are one of a kind and you have the promise of your Father: He says He will never leave nor forsake you. So often, we tend to view another person's lawn as being greener than ours. But the truth is, every blade of green grass is nurtured with dirt fertilized by manure. The same is true about our lives. People whose lives look greener are those who have taken the dirt that life has given them to fertilize their grass. Everyone has dirt, but the difference is what we do with our dirt.

There are people who are sitting in their dirt complaining about how unfair life is and how everyone else is doing so well. This category of people wish that they were on the other side where the grass is greener—where there is no dirt, they assume. But the grass is never greener on the other side, it is only greener where it has been watered.

The other group of people are those who use the dirt they have to transform their lives for the better. Nothing can grow without dirt. Your dirt could be the loss of a loved one, a divorce, a health challenge, a traumatic experience, or an unfair treatment that left you feeling hopeless. Whatever the case may be, your dirt can become the very thing that will transform your life for good, if you let it.

After my divorce, I sat around my dirt for a while, complaining about how unfair the whole situation was. It wasn't until I began to study the lives of those who appeared to have greener pastures that I began to realize that all of the successful people we know or have heard about have learned to use their dirt to their advantage.

Oprah Winfrey is a force to be reckoned with and her accomplishments are phenomenal. But what people may not know is that her life was full of dirt as a growing child. She was born to a teenage mother, and at a very young age, she was repeatedly molested. She was emotionally wounded to a point that she was sent to a juvenile detention home where she was denied admission because all the beds were occupied. As if that was not enough, she got pregnant as a teenager and lost her baby in infancy. She then moved in with her father who was committed to giving her the best life possible. It was at this point that she began to use her dirt to fertilize her life, and she has continued to flourish ever since. Her dominance in the entertainment industry is profound and her name has become synonymous with success. Every woman I know is inspired by her accomplishments, but I don't know how many are willing to use the shameful things that have happened in their lives for their own good.

Pat Smith is yet another person who used her dirt to fertilize her life. Pat was the first black woman to become Miss Virginia in 1993, and in 1994 she was first runner-up to Miss USA. She married an actor, Martin Lawrence, and two years later, she was divorced. What looked on the outside like a fabulous life was crumbling to pieces. She felt ashamed about her divorce, but the shame only pulled her closer in relationship to God. She lost her mother at a young age to breast cancer. She battled with finding her purpose in life and often saw herself as a failure, despite the many accomplishments she had won crowns and trophies for. Today, she is married to Emmitt Smith, former Dallas Cowboy player, and they are happily married. They both own a charity organization, and they are both fulfilling their destiny. Pat has an online clothing store and she is the author of the book so perfectly entitled, Second Chances.

Another person who has used her dirt to fertilize her life is Pastor Sarah Jakes Roberts, daughter of the renowned preacher, Bishop T.D. Jakes. Growing up, Sarah had a hard time trying to fit in at the church as a preacher's kid. There was so much expectation placed on her, and she didn't measure up to any of them. She had a baby at age 14, and in an attempt to make things right, she got married at age 19 only to be divorced by age 25. Things only went from bad to worse for Sarah, and as a way of escape, she began writing an online blog about her experiences. In that season, she wrote a book entitled, *Lost and Found*. A few years after her divorce, she met Pastor Toure Roberts, and they are happily married today. Sarah had a rough start, but now she is an author, speaker, and preacher—amongst many other things. This goes to show that where you start is not as important as where you end up.

We can draw inspiration from these women's stories. Here's my take: we don't have to wish we were on the other side where we think the grass is greener. Your grass can become greener if you water and fertilize it with your own dirt. Life is what we make of it. **You determine your outcome, and may it never be said that you quit.** We all know the famous phrase: quitters don't win, and winners don't quit.

FIGHT

We have already established the fact that life is a battle and that no one comes out of it without bruises and scars. There's nothing like a scratch-free life because it doesn't exist. You are like a boxer in the ring of life. When life gets tough, you've got to strap on your boxing gloves and fight back.

I have watched a few boxing games in my life, and I have yet to see a boxer who wins a match without a bruise or a scratch. Most of them come out with busted lips, bruises, sprains, dislocations, and possible concussions. Pretty intense, right? Life is the same way. I don't know of anyone who has fought the good fight without scars.

Paul understood this when he said, "I have fought the good fight, I have finished the race, I have kept the faith. Finally, there is laid up for me the crown of righteousness, which the Lord, the righteous Judge, will give to me on that Day, and not to me only but also to all who have loved His appearing" (2 Timothy 4:7-8 NKJV).

You cannot be crowned if you are not willing to fight and win. **You must fight for your place in life because you will not be crowned for standing on the sidelines. You are more likely to win the prize if you get into the game and fight. Fight for your faith, fight for your marriage, fight for your health, fight for your peace, fight for your happiness, fight for your family, fight for your dreams, fight for your children, fight for your freedom, fight for your sanity, and fight for your life.** We are not in a fight against people, rather we are in a fight against the things that threaten to take us out. The scripture is very clear on this when it says, "For we do not wrestle against flesh and blood, but against principalities, against powers, against the rulers of the darkness of this age, against spiritual hosts of wickedness in the heavenly places" (Ephesians 6:12 NKJV).

What are you battling with? What is threatening your peace? I battled with anger for years. I was angry because I felt the people that had mistreated me didn't get the punishment they deserved. I directed my anger toward them and utilized every opportunity I had to make them look bad. I did this for a while, but it was very exhausting. I realized I was expending my energy in the wrong place, so I began to look at the good side of what had happened to me.

Remember perception is everything. You can choose to see your life as good or bad. No matter how bad a situation is, there is always something good to be found if we look with a different lens. I began to perceive my situation differently and I thought, if I hadn't suffered injustice in the hands of my abusers, I wouldn't have discovered my true self. I wouldn't have become the person I am today. Maybe, I wouldn't have written this book. I certainly wouldn't have learned how to forgive.

Forgiveness is not a gift, it's a choice. I had to fight against my desire to stay angry with those who had hurt me. It was a tough decision to make, but I would have continued to destroy myself had I not made the choice to forgive. It's not your job to teach anyone a lesson; life will teach everyone what they need to know. Your fight is not against people, but against the principalities and powers of this world—the things that are robbing you of your peace, joy, and happiness.

Whatever that thing may be for you, it's time to wage a war against it. And just like the boxer in the ring, you may have your lips busted, your eyes blacked out, your shoulder dislocated, your leg amputated, or your heart broken—but you must fight the good fight.

If you desire to have nothing short of what God has in store for you then you must be willing to give Him all that you've got. You cannot give less than what you have and expect all that you want.

When Jesus was asked what the greatest commandment was, Jesus replied, "Love the Lord your God with all your heart, with all your soul, and with all your mind" (Matthew 22:37-38 NIV). That's a lot of "all" if you ask me. We tend to pick and choose what we give God. We can give him this, but not that. Giving God our all is not a convenient thing to do because we always want to feel like we are in charge. Beyond our need to feel in control, giving up our all requires trust.

We can only give God everything when we trust Him. No wonder scripture instructs us to trust the Lord with all our heart (Proverbs 3:5-6). Again, we see God asking us to give Him all we've got.

The story of Abraham and Isaac is a fitting example in this case. God asked Abraham to offer his son—his only promised son, Isaac, as a burnt offering at Mount Moriah. Isaac was all Abraham had. Abraham could have easily held back his all, but he didn't because he trusted God more than anything else. When Isaac asked his father where the sacrifice was, Abraham responded, "My son, God will provide for Himself the lamb for a burnt offering" (Genesis 22:8 KJV).

That is trust! Abraham was certain that God would provide the lamb for the sacrifice, and He did. And because Abraham trusted God with all that he had, God blessed him with all he could ever ask for.

"By Myself I have sworn, says the Lord because you have done this thing, and have not withheld your son, your only son— blessing I will bless you, and multiplying I will multiply your descendants as the stars of the heaven and as the sand which is on the seashore; and your descendants shall possess the gate of their enemies. In your seed all the nations of the earth shall be blessed, because you have obeyed My voice" (Genesis 22:16-18 NKJV).

Sometimes life leaves us broken, hardened, and unable to trust anyone—but the only one who can restore us is God. However, God cannot restore what you won't commit to His hands. We've got to be willing to surrender all—every part of us—for God to begin His work in us.

Just as God responds to us when we give our all, life does the same when we give our all. When you give your all toward your spouse, your children, your career, or your dreams—life will have no option but to yield its all to you. Whatever your hands find to do, do it with all that you've got. Where you are now may not be where you want to be, but you've got to be faithful where you are.

Think of yourself as a builder who desires to build a wall. A wall cannot be built overnight, but you can commit to laying a block every day. The secret to building a strong fortress is laying one block as perfectly as a block can be laid, one at a time. Lay each block as though your life depends on it—and it does. If you stack your blocks carelessly, they will come crumbling down. But if you lay one block at a time, precisely and accurately, you will have an unshakeable wall in no time.

I have realized that it takes the same amount of time and effort to do something properly as it does to do something carelessly. So, why not choose to do it properly? Don't let life's experiences make you a mediocre version of yourself. Instead, commit to living a life of excellence and credibility. Let your work speak for itself. Let your word be your bond. Let your name be synonymous with integrity. Make room in your heart for offense, because offense will come by the truckload as you continue to live in this world.

In other words, learn to forgive people even before they offend you. Offense is part of human nature, so it is wise to be prepared for it. It's ignorant to assume offense will not come, but we can learn to guard our hearts against hurt by practicing these things ahead of time. Start by treating others the way you would like to be treated. This is not to say you will never offend anyone. But when you do offend others, you will find yourself apologizing quickly.

In the same vein, if someone offends you, let them know. So often, we expect other people to apologize for something they probably aren't even aware of. If you have been hurt, let the other party know by telling them in a loving way. Attacking or judging them will only worsen the situation. Don't say things that would make them look bad either. Remember they are not the problem, their actions are.

This is very critical because the way we handle our relationships determine the quality of our lives. If we don't learn how to handle offense, we will end up frustrated, angry, and lonely. Now, this is not easy to practice, but it is a very healthy way to live. Everyone, at one point or another, has experienced a heartbreak because of what someone else said or did. Their actions may have left you feeling unworthy, selfish, edgy, intolerant, and even aggressive toward others.

I went through what I call "the most horrendous time of my life" when I was living with my ex-husband. I had no idea I would be writing about forgiveness because I thought it would be impossible to do. It's easy to forgive minor offenses like when someone bumps into you in the hallway. But when the offense is huge, we tend to hold on to it for much longer than we should.

Regardless of the magnitude of the offense, forgiveness is a choice. I made a choice to forgive my offender because I wanted to live a healthy life. Unforgiveness is toxic and it will keep you bound if you refuse to let go. Unforgiveness is like building a cage for someone else, only to discover that you are the one in it. Learning to be more gracious toward others is the best gift we can give ourselves. Forgiveness is not about the person who offended you—it is all about you.

Here's what Jesus said about forgiveness in Matthew 6:14 (NKJV): "For if you forgive men their trespasses, your heavenly Father will also forgive you. But if you do not forgive men their trespasses, neither will your Father forgive your trespasses."

Our forgiveness from the Father is tied to our forgiveness toward others. Don't let someone else's offense deprive you of the grace and love of your Father. It's not worth it. Let it go! When you make room in your heart for offense, you will not take it to heart when people offend you. You will begin to act like Christ, who is slow to anger and abounding in mercy.

In addition, you will have a healthier heart. Imagine you have a catheter attached to your heart and the job of the catheter is to remove any and all offenses as they come in. Without the catheter, offenses will build up in your heart and eventually threaten your life. That's not worth it!

You might be wondering or asking, "But what happens to the offender if we forgive?" And here's what I will say to you: let God deal with them. You do your part in forgiving them—and let them and the offense go. God is clear about the responsibility of revenge when He says, "Do not take revenge, my dear friends, but leave room for God's wrath, for it is written: 'It is mine to avenge; I will repay,' says the Lord" (Romans 12:19 NIV).

Life may have been unfair to you. People may have treated you badly. But we serve a just God, and He will decree justice on your behalf.

7
USE YOUR OWN ARMOR

God has uniquely equipped each one of us with what we need to win our own battles. You will only win your battle if you use what you have been given. Trying to use someone else's armor will only result in failure. David defeated Goliath using his own weapons: a stone and a slingshot. His weapons didn't look fancy, but they were effective. Don't use the weapons others are recommending for you simply because they look fancy. Use what you have been given—they will get the job done!

Weapons only work in the hands of the owner. If you have not been trained to use a certain weapon, why use it on the day of battle? Use what you have tested and proven to work for you. Prior to the fight between David and Goliath, King Saul placed his armor on David, but it didn't fit him.

"So Saul clothed David with his armor, and he put a bronze helmet on his head; he also clothed him with a coat of mail. David fastened his sword to his armor and tried to walk, for he had not tested them. And David said to Saul, "I cannot walk with these, for I have not tested them." So David took them off. Then he took his staff in his hand; and he chose for himself five smooth stones from the brook, and put them in a shepherd's bag, in a pouch which he had, and his sling was in his hand. And he drew near to the Philistine" (1 Samuel 17:38-40 NKJV).

As soon as David picked up his weapons, his confidence came alive and he approached the giant to fight him. David had tested his weapons on bears and lions, so he knew how to work them. He knew they were effective. Goliath was furious when he saw young David approaching the battlefield with his own weapons. Goliath taunted David saying, "Come to me, and I will give your flesh to the birds of the air and the beasts of the field!" (1 Samuel 17:44 NKJV).

Here's another lesson to take home: never fight your enemy on their terms. Goliath was a foot soldier who was trained to fight close combats with swords, so he asked David to come close to him because that was the only way he knew how to fight. David, on the other hand, was a slinger. He had been trained to strike from a distance, and he approached Goliath with that understanding. David fought Goliath and won by using his own weapons and his own strategy.

Every battle requires a strategy to win. What is your strategy to win? David prepared himself for battle in advance by practicing as he protected his sheep in private. Some of us are passively waiting for a big opportunity to strike. But success only happens when preparation meets opportunity. You've got to prepare for the moment, the opportunity, and the battle. You cannot afford to show up at the battlefield unprepared because your nerves will fail you.

David was sure he would defeat Goliath because he came prepared. Now, it's important to point out that preparation alone will not get the job done. Belief is a vital requirement for victory. David believed that God was with him. These were his exact words in 1 Samuel 17:37 (NKJV): "The Lord, who delivered me from the paw of the lion and from the paw of the bear, He will deliver me from the hand of this Philistine." David was sure that God was on his side and his belief gave him victory.

Some of us are preparing for battle but we don't believe we can have the victory. You've got to believe you can win before you approach the battlefield. You cannot approach the battle with a defeated mentality and expect to win. The battle is won first in your mind and then in your life. Your belief will give you the courage to step out and fight. Once David chose his weapons, he approached Goliath. There's a strange confidence that comes upon you when you are wearing your armor. This kind of confidence will make you confront your enemy, even when they look bigger than you. David was not afraid of Goliath's size because he was wearing his own armor. His confidence would have been shaken if he wore Saul's armor to the battle. Be confident in what you possess. People will try to talk you out of your purpose, but when you are grounded in your faith, you will defy every opposition. I pray that your head will be stronger than that of your enemy, in Jesus' name.

Now, don't think your enemy will show up without a strategy. Goliath's strategy was to shout David down. He began cursing David by his gods saying he would give David's flesh to the birds and the beasts of the field. Goliath's intention was to intimidate David, but his strategy only fueled David's confidence. Your enemy is not as powerful as they appear. They seek to instill fear in you by roaring like a giant. Rejoice when they appear to be bigger than you are because the bigger they are, the harder they fall. Learn to use the enemy's threat to your own advantage because greater is He that is in you than he that is in the world (1 John 4:4). Your God is greater than the giant standing in front of you.

ENEMIES

In life, you cannot have friends without enemies. You can't have one without the other. If you have one, then you will have the other. That is the reality we live in and to think that you will only have friends is naive and unattainable.

If Jesus had enemies then you can be sure that you will also have enemies along the way. Enemies are people that cannot stand to see you blessed. In modern times, we call them haters. Haters are simply enemies in disguise. Psalms 23:5 (NKJV) states clearly that God "will prepare a table for you in the presence of your enemies." God is aware of your enemies, and He has promised to bless you in spite of their presence in your life.

Enemies are everywhere. You don't have to invite them into your life, they will just show up unannounced. Remember, when the Lord asked Satan where he was coming from, He said, "From going to and fro on the earth, and from walking back and forth on it" (Job 1:7 NKJV). The devil, who is your enemy, is roaring around like a lion looking for someone to destroy. The devil has come to steal, kill, and destroy. If the enemy's plan is to destroy you, then your plan should be to destroy him first. To crush him completely.

David understood this principle because after he killed Goliath, he went on to cut off the giant's head. This is what it means to crush the enemy completely. Goliath was already dead after David struck him with the stone, so cutting off his head wasn't exactly necessary. But David did it anyway. The devil will not leave you half dead; therefore, you've got to be as brutal as the devil would be if you were his prey.

Anything or anyone that is threatening your existence is your enemy. We have been instructed by God to love our enemies and to pray for those who hate us. However, when the enemy is committed to taking you out, you must be committed to taking them out first. You cannot be cute about eliminating your enemy. God is committed to wiping out your enemies. Why do you think the Bible refers to God as a "consuming fire" or "the Lion of the tribe of Judah" in Hebrews 12:29 and Revelation 5:5? It is because God is committed to eliminating those who are attempting to eliminate you.

Our weapons of warfare are not carnal but are mighty to the pulling down of strongholds. Any high thing that has exalted itself against the name of our Lord Jesus must be pulled down (2 Corinthian 10:4-5). Any mouth that is cursing you must be silenced by the power in the name of Jesus. Any evil hand that is pointing in your direction must wither in the name of Jesus. Any evil eye that is looking in your direction must be blinded in the name of Jesus. Any sickness in your body must bow to the healing power in the name of Jesus. Any man or woman who has vowed that you will not see the light of day will die in your place in the name of Jesus. Whatever is threatening your peace will be threatened in the name of Jesus.

Whatever is overwhelming you will be overwhelmed by the presence of the Most High God in Jesus' name. God is committed to saving us from the hand of those who are stronger than us. Isaiah 49:25-26 (NKJV) says, "But thus says the Lord, Even the captives of the mighty shall be taken away, and the prey of the terrible be delivered; for I will contend with him who contends with you, and I will save your children. I will feed those who oppress you with their own flesh, and they shall be drunk with their own blood as with sweet wine. All flesh shall know that I, the Lord, am your Savior, and your Redeemer, the Mighty One of Jacob."

That is the God we serve! He has promised to protect you at all costs, and I dare your enemy to bring it on.

MAKE GOD THE PRIORITY IN YOUR LIFE

God is the only one worthy of taking the first place in our lives. Anything else we attempt to put before Him will fade away. There is a void in every one of us that can only be filled by the One who made us. God wants us to acknowledge Him in all we do. He wants to occupy the first place in our lives. He wants us to make Him our first priority.

Sometimes we make the mistake of putting our careers, marriages, spouses, relationships, children, friends, pursuit of wealth, or personal ambitions before God. But the moment we do this, we give up God's best for us in exchange for what we think we should have. God's ways are always better than ours. Unfortunately, we tend to realize this truth after a series of unpleasant experiences.

There's nothing we have today that we did not receive from God so what makes us think that we can put any of those things before Him and succeed? God is very clear about His place in our lives and we see that in Exodus 20:1-6 (NKJV):

And God spoke all these words, saying: "I am the Lord your God, who brought you out of the land of Egypt, out of the house of bondage. You shall have no other gods before Me. You shall not make for yourself a carved image—any likeness of anything that is in heaven above, or that is in the earth beneath, or that is in the water under the earth; you shall not bow down to them nor serve them. For I, your God, am a jealous God, visiting the iniquity of the fathers upon the children to the third and fourth generations of those who hate Me, but showing mercy to thousands, to those who love Me and keep My commandments."

Now, God is not suggesting that we put Him first, He is commanding us to do so. We have been redeemed through the precious blood of Jesus Christ, so we don't own ourselves. We belong to God and He belongs to us. Nothing is more precious in the eyes of God than you and me, the ones He made in His image and likeness.

Discipline is not negotiable if you want to win in life. I hear a lot of people say things like, "I know I should lose some weight," or "I know I should treat people better," or "I know I should be more committed to my goals," or "I know I should go back to school," and so on. The problem is, they haven't learned how to turn their should into a must, so they simply acknowledge what they should do but they don't do them. Why? Because they have yet to make discipline a major force in their life.

"For the moment all discipline seems painful rather than pleasant, but later it yields the peaceful fruit of righteousness to those who have been trained by it" (Hebrews 12:11 ESV).

Discipline is not fun, but it will bring you all the fun you want in the end. Muhammad Ali once said, "I hated every minute of training, but I said, 'Don't quit. Suffer now and live the rest of your life as a champion.'" Ali understood the force of discipline and he was indeed a champion.

It takes discipline to live like a champion. People love titles, but they dislike the discipline required to get them. If you want to be a champion, then you must align yourself with what it takes to become a champion. It takes discipline to program your mind to believe you are a champion. However, it takes greater discipline to live and train like a champion. Champions train even when it hurts. They understand the pain of discipline is nothing compared to the joy of victory.

I recall, shortly after my divorce, some friends were telling me I needed to get out into the world and socialize. Honestly, I wanted to, but I chose to yield to the greater call upon my life that demanded I deprive myself of certain things. Champions don't go with popular opinion. If you don't have a plan for your life, people will create one for you. When everyone else thought I was missing out on social life, I was training myself to become a champion in life. I began by reprogramming my mind to believe that my dreams were possible. Real, lasting change starts from within.

People may not see the value in what you are doing now, but if you stay committed, your work will speak for itself. **Champions are not superior to others, they are just different.** They work while others play. They are committed to doing the things others will only speak about and not act upon. They endure the pain of discipline because they know it's only temporary. Champions change whatever they don't like around them and if they cannot change it, they change their attitude toward it. That's what sets champions apart.

Champions are not conformers, they are transformers. They are not followers, they are leaders. Like the Bible says, "Do not be conformed to this world, but be transformed by the renewing of your mind, that you may prove what is that good and acceptable and perfect will of God" (Romans 12:2 NKJV).

Champions are constantly looking for ways to become better. They never settle for where they are. They don't reside in their comfort zone—they are comfortable with being in an unfamiliar territory. They are coachable, they accept correction, and they are willing to volunteer their time to help others. And all of these attributes are possible because of one thing: discipline.

TRAITS OF A WINNER

Refusing to conform to popular belief is a distinct trait of a winner. Winners are not conformers, they are transformers. Winners do not do the things that are convenient, popular, comfortable or widely acceptable. They dare to do what others will not attempt to do.

Consider the story of Daniel, Shadrach, Meshach, and Abednego who refused to defile themselves with the king's food and drinks. Instead, they ate vegetables and drank water for ten days while the others ate what was offered to them. At the end of ten days, Daniel and his friends were stronger than those who indulged. This goes to show that you cannot do something differently and not have a different result.

Quit traveling the same path you have been on for years expecting a different outcome. If you are not seeing the desired results you want, then it's time for you to begin on a new path—a path that is seldom traveled. Many will travel on the highway of life, but few are disciplined enough to resist taking the most common way. These few will be the winners in life. Winners travel the narrow road of life. They will endure a little deprivation, so they can enjoy freedom for the rest of their lives.

Winners often appear to be super humans because of the results they are able to produce. The Bible speaks of Daniel and his friends in Daniel 1:17 (NKJV) saying, "As for these four young men, God gave them knowledge and skill in all literature and wisdom; and Daniel had understanding in all visions and dreams." When you commit to living like a winner, God will give you uncommon wisdom that will make you a wonder to your world.

The good news is, anyone can commit to traveling the narrow path of life. You don't need to have any special trait to live like a winner—you just have to abstain from popular belief. Winners stand up for the truth, even when their lives are threatened. Shadrach, Meshach, and Abednego refused to worship the gold image that King Nebuchadnezzar set up—even when their lives were being threatened—because it was in direct opposition to God's law. Winners do not retreat when threatened. They stand their ground no matter what.

When King Nebuchadnezzar threatened that he was going to throw these Hebrew men into the burning furnace for not worshipping the gold image, they stood their ground and refused to bow. Shadrach, Meshach, and Abednego answered the king saying, "O Nebuchadnezzar, we have no need to answer you in this matter. If that is the case, our God whom we serve is able to deliver us from the burning fiery furnace, and He will deliver us from your hand, O king. But if not, let it be known to you, O king, that we do not serve your gods, nor will we worship the gold image which you have set up" (Daniel 3:16-18 NKJV).

Winners are unshakeable. They don't waver, because they believe their approach will work. Winners are believers. They trust that a different approach will always result in a different outcome. Transformation starts in the mind. If you can renew your mind, you can transform your life.

What belief have you held in your mind that is holding you back from becoming all you can be? Victory begins in your mind and so does defeat. You cannot rise above your thinking. You cannot assume defeat and have victory. Our thoughts will eventually shape our lives because we often act on our dominant thoughts.

Everything we have ever achieved or failed to achieve started with a thought. Our thoughts are powerful; therefore, it is very important that we think healthy, positive thoughts. We can learn to feed our minds with positive information through the words we read, speak, and hear. **Beliefs come from repeated affirmation, but affirmation without discipline is delusion.** It's not enough to say repeatedly, "I am a winner." You must match your positive affirmation with the required discipline.

Take a good look at your life. Are you doing the things

that winners do? Winners have a blueprint for their lives and they work tirelessly to achieve what they want. Winners live life on purpose. No one is going to walk into your life and give you purpose. You've got to discover your own purpose in life. Your life will assume a new meaning once your purpose is established.

Life happens to everyone, but what separates winners from the rest of the world is their perception. Winners focus on the good in every situation. They don't just talk about what they want, but they act on what they talk about. Nothing happens without action. Many people think good thoughts, but they don't act on them, so they produce nothing. Action is the key to making things happen. Thinking alone won't do it. Your thoughts must be backed with action.

Winners take the most action. Do today what you know you can do today—don't wait until tomorrow. Endure the pain of discipline so you can enjoy the pleasure of winning. Winners are just like you and me. They lose but they don't quit. They face rejection and disappointment, but they don't stop moving.

Life is like running a marathon: it's not about how fast you can run from the start to the finish line, it's about keeping your pace, learning how to avoid injury, and enjoying the journey. Learning how to avoid injuries in life is what a winner does with finesse. Winners get knocked down several times just like anyone else running life's race, but they have learned to rise back up each time they fall. They may suffer betrayal along the way, but they learn to trust again. They may make mistakes, but they refuse to be bound by the fear of failure.

This is what the winning life is all about! You learn, then you learn, and then you keep learning. It's living life with a different approach and a positive mindset. Remember you were born to win in life. You are a winner!

TAKE DOMINION

8
GRACE AND GUT

Grace is God's gift to us. Grace is received, not earned. No one could ever earn grace—even if they tried. Ephesians 2:8 (NKJV) says, "For by grace you have been saved through faith, and that not of yourselves; it is the gift of God."

God's grace is freely given to anyone who is willing to receive it. Grace goes hand in hand with gut. It takes gut to receive grace. Gut represents boldness. No wonder Hebrews 4:16 (NKJV) says, "Let us therefore come boldly to the throne of grace, that we may obtain mercy and find grace to help in time of need." Therefore, to receive grace, we need gut. We cannot receive grace if we feel guilt and shame. We ought to believe that we have been redeemed by the precious blood of Jesus Christ and that we are worthy of God's gift called grace.

Grace finds us worthy even when our past says we are unworthy. It is natural for us to feel guilty when we do something wrong, but our heavenly Father has already paid the price for our wrongdoing. Apostle Paul is a great example of the expression of God's grace. Prior to his encounter with God in Acts Chapter 9, Paul, formerly known as Saul, was a sinner who persecuted Christians everywhere. But Paul believed in the redemptive power of Jesus and he received the grace of God upon his life to become a missionary. His acknowledgment of God's grace resulted in the writings of the majority of the New Testament.

Paul acknowledged receiving the grace of God when he spoke to the people of Corinth saying, "For I delivered to you first of all that which I also received: that Christ died for our sins according to the Scriptures, and that He was buried, and that He rose again the third day according to the Scriptures... For I am the least of the apostles, am not worthy to be called an apostle, because I persecuted the church of God. But by the grace of God I am what I am, and His grace toward me was not in vain; but I labored more abundantly than they all, yet not I, but the grace of God which was with me" (1 Corinthians 15:3-10 NKJV).

Paul was not worthy of God's grace, but he chose to receive it because of his belief in Jesus Christ. We can make a choice to receive what our Father has already provided for us and avoid the pain of living in shame. After my divorce, I was so embarrassed that I felt unworthy of love. As I began to accept what had happened in my previous marriage, I was reminded that my Father loves me unconditionally. He loves me just the way I am. His love knows no bounds. He is mindful of me and nothing will separate me from His love. I realized God was not ashamed of me and the shame I felt was an indication that I had not received the grace of God.

It takes humility to receive something you cannot earn. **We have been taught to earn everything we've got, but grace is an exception.** It's no surprise that James 4:6 (NKJV) says, "God resists the proud but gives grace to the humble." Those who are humble have chosen to receive what they cannot earn by themselves, and I believe God is moved by that.

If you feel unworthy of God's grace because of what

happened in your past, here's what you have to do: Believe in your heart that Jesus died and rose for your sins, confess with your mouth that Jesus is Lord, and come to Him boldly so you can receive His mercy and grace. That is the only way out.

It's okay to admit that you don't have all the answers to the issues of life. As a matter of fact, no one does. Take the pressure off of yourself, and let God unravel the things you cannot understand. A scripture that encourages me and gives me peace is Romans 8:28 (KJV) saying, "We know that all things work together for good to them that love God, to them who are the called according to his purpose." When I find myself perplexed about an issue in my life, I remind myself that all things will work together for my good. I have learned to accept the fact that I don't have all the answers. Only God has all the answers, so I trust Him with all the issues in my life.

Our walk with God requires us to trust Him in everything we do. Trust is born out of a relationship. You cannot trust someone you don't know. Our personal relationship with God gives us the opportunity to know His very nature. Psalms 18:30 (NKJV) says, "As for God, His way is perfect: the word of the Lord is proven: He is a shield to all those that trust in Him." God's word reveals to us who He is, and the more of the Word we have in us, the more we know about Him.

Trust is a product of faith in the Word, which is God Himself. Therefore, knowing God equals knowing His Word. Scripture says that God magnified His Word above His name (Psalms 138: 2). What does that tell us? God's Word is unbreakable, it's unshakeable, it's infallible, and it's everlasting. What a great God we serve!

The night I left my ex-husband, I had no money on hand, no money in the bank, no personal or joint property—I had nothing but faith. I had to trust that God would take care of me, my child, and my mother. The first night, I drove to my job and we slept in the parking lot inside of the van my ex-husband had purchased. The next morning, two of my coworkers took my mother and my son to their apartment while I washed my face and got ready for work. A week later, I got paid and moved my family into my first apartment.

I didn't have it all figured out that first night, but I trusted the One who knows the end from the beginning. God will always make a way for you when you trust in Him. You don't need to know exactly what your next move will be—all you have to do is trust in God because He always comes through. Sometimes we are afraid of the unknown, the things that may happen if we make the next move. But guess what? Life will happen regardless, so rather than have life happen to you—make life happen for you. Trust your instinct. It's your God-given gut. When you feel it in your gut—go for it. The outcome may not be the one you expect, but the outcome will always be in your favor.

After I moved into my apartment, I was faced with even more challenges. I learned that Joyce Meyer's famously quoted phrase was certainly true: "New level, new devil." The higher you go, the greater the challenges you face. When people learned of my separation, everyone seemed to have an opinion about a marriage that they had no prior knowledge about. Some accused me of depriving my ex-husband of his rights to see his son. Others said I should have remained in my marriage no matter what—as it was for better, and for worse.

It is interesting how people become marriage counselors the moment they hear someone's marriage is in trouble. I agree, marriage is for better and for worse, but when your life is in danger—you ought to call for help and flee for safety. I was naïve, and I allowed people's opinions to pull me in different directions. In an attempt to please the many voices that were speaking about my situation, I decided to contact my ex-husband just before our son's first birthday. After the party, my ex-husband asked to move into my one-bedroom apartment, and I agreed because I wanted to prove all the naysayers wrong.

I became an actor in my own marriage. It appeared as though everything was going well, but in reality, things were falling apart. I wore a mask on the outside, pretending my marriage was working, while I was dying on the inside. I was awakened to the fact that we were headed for destruction. Not everyone agreed with my decision to be separated from an abuser, but I made the choice to tune out the voices on the outside, so I could hear the still voice within me. The moment I stopped worrying about what other people thought about me, the easier it was for me to process my thoughts and to map out an action plan for my life.

People will judge you based on their own perception, but perception is relative. Everyone is entitled to their own opinion, but like Les Brown once said, "Someone's opinion of you does not have to become your reality." When people judge you, you don't have to defend yourself or pick a fight with them. You simply need to push the ignore button and keep moving forward. You must have tough skin to go through life unscathed because you will certainly meet with harsh critics and false accusers along the way.

It's important to know that not everyone will support your cause and you've got to be willing to move forward without some people. People come into our lives during certain seasons for specific reasons. Every relationship in your life must have a purpose. Don't keep people in your life for sentimental reasons. Any relationship that is not making you better is not worth maintaining.

Quit trying to keep up with everybody. It costs too much to do that! Learn to surround yourself with people who are growing in two major areas: those who are growing spiritually and those who are growing economically. Partner with people who inspire you to become better. When you are surrounded by purposeful relationships, you will have no time to entertain critics. Make no mistake—you will be criticized no matter what you do. The only people who are exempt from criticism are those who do nothing and therefore become nothing. If you want something great out of life, then you've got to be ready to face criticism. Learn to use criticism as fuel for your purpose. Let criticism motivate you to become better. Don't get offended when people criticize you, get excited because your actions are not going unnoticed.

Don't quit stoking your fire because of what someone else says or thinks. Don't be a people pleaser—become a God pleaser. Apostle Paul understood this point and in Galatians

1:10 (NIV) he said, "Am I now trying to win the approval of human beings, or of God? Or am I trying to please people? If I were still trying to please people, I would not be a servant of Christ." In other words, you cannot be a pleaser of men and become all that God has destined for you to become. The people you allow to influence your life will do one of two things: push you toward your destiny or pull you away from your destiny. You don't get to choose certain things in life, but you do get to choose your friends. Choose wisely and live freely.

When we've been hurt by someone, the natural response is to want to hurt them back or at least make them feel the pain they have caused us. Sometimes we will even go so far as trying to straighten them out. If you have tried that in the past, you know by now that it doesn't work. **Trying to fix anyone other than yourself is an impossible mission. You cannot fix anyone you did not create, and the last time I checked, you and I haven't created anyone.** God is the only one who can fix us because He made us. No matter how badly someone may have hurt you, you don't have the power to change them. But you do have the power to change the way you treat them.

Don't fall into the temptation of treating them the way they really deserve. That would be retaliating and that is not the solution to fixing them. Retaliation is succumbing to the level of hurting people because they have hurt you. Whereas choosing to forgive those who have hurt you is rising above the hurt and building your character. Now, this is not easy to do—especially if the hurt is deep. But it is possible to forgive, no matter how deep the cut.

I struggled with forgiving my ex-husband for a while, and during that time I wanted to repay him for what he had done to me. I wanted to make him feel the pain that I felt. As I began to lean into God's call upon my life, I knew I had to make peace with the part of me that sought revenge. It became clear to me that I had to rise above the hurt and step into a place where I could not only forgive what had already been done but also what would be done in the future.

To get to this point, you've got to be willing to let go of your rights to justify your unforgiveness. Let God be the judge by surrendering your broken heart to Him. He will not despise your broken heart. He is man enough to feel your pain, and He is God enough to restore your brokenness. Rather than trying to make the other person pay for what they have done, you will be better off working on yourself to achieve wholeness. Your journey toward becoming whole should be your priority. What others decide to do with their own lives is totally up to them. It is not your responsibility to fix or punish them. It is your responsibility to decide to live above what they have done.

There will be many opportunities in life but not every opportunity is right for you. Just because an opportunity appears to work for everyone around you, does not mean it will work for you. You have a unique path that is distinct from any other. No wonder 1 Corinthians 10:23 (ESV) says, "All things are lawful for me, but not all things are helpful; all things are lawful for me, but not all things build up."

Shortly after my divorce, I was so desperate to change my financial situation that I embarked on a home-based business that virtually everyone around me was doing. I thought because it was working for them, it would also work for me. I was puzzled when the business didn't amount to much, despite all the effort I put into it. Sometimes we can run the risk of measuring effort and energy instead of results. I was very busy running the business, but I wasn't producing enough results to show for it. Busyness doesn't equal business. It's possible to be busy and not productive. If you've ever put so much into something only to receive so little, then I bet you know the feeling—it's awful.

It took me a while to admit that my approach toward the business was faulty from the start. Making money was my primary motivation, and no endeavor can be sustained if money is the only incentive. Another mistake I made with the business was starting it because of the success I had seen other people have with it. Lesson learned: never do something simply because others are doing it. Only pursue what you are passionate about because you have a conviction that it is leading you toward your destiny—your ultimate destination.

This is not to say that your path toward destiny is going to be without failure and disappointment. However, when you are on the right path, you are better equipped to withstand whatever comes your way. And if you are wondering whether or not you should embark on your next move, consider Philippians 4:8-9 (NKJV): "Finally, brethren, whatever things are true, whatever things are noble, whatever things are just, whatever things are pure, whatever things are lovely, whatever things are of good report, if there is any virtue and if there is anything praiseworthy—meditate on these things. The things which you learned and received and heard and saw in me, these do, and the God of peace will be with you."

There couldn't be a better guide on how to choose between opportunities as they present themselves. Life's choices can be overwhelming, but having a sound checklist like the one above can help weed out what is not helpful for us. There is a purpose for your life and your purpose should drive your choices. The key here is making choices that are purposeful. There are a lot of good ideas but not all of them are purposeful. Your choices must align with your purpose.

Now, this idea is contrary to popular belief because we are taught to go for anything we want. The danger with that is this: there are no boundaries when you go for anything, and boundaries are necessary for a healthy life. We need to be intentional about the choices we make. Choices come in the form of daily decisions that gradually shape our lives, so we ought to take them seriously. Don't make decisions out of peer pressure, popular opinion, or sentiments; rather, make decisions based on knowledge, reason, and purpose.

Life yields to persistence. One strike cannot and will not get the job done. One shot is not enough to achieve your goals. Success happens when people are willing to try several times until they achieve their desired result. You cannot go to the gym once and quit the next day, simply because you don't look like the image on the cover of a sport's magazine. In order to look like the image you have envisioned for yourself, you've got to work until it happens. You've got to be willing to take countless shots at life.

Persistence is the secret weapon that compels life to

give up what it has for you. Imagine you are a woodcutter standing in front a giant tree with an axe in your hand. Your assignment is to cut the tree down, using the axe you've been given. You have the right tool to bring the tree down, but the tree will not come down after a strike or two. It may not even come down after the hundredth strike or even the thousandth strike. You've got to keep striking the tree until it falls. The key word is: until.

The difference between the person who stops after a few strikes and the one who strikes until the tree falls is persistence. Now, it is important to note that the tree will only come down when we strike the same spot repeatedly. Most of us are striking, but we are not striking the same spot. Our tendency can be to hover around several things without focusing on one thing at a time. We are busy, but we are not productive.

The key to producing positive results is narrowing our activities down to specifics for effectiveness. The strike that brings the tree down is not the ultimate strike; rather, the culmination of the previous strikes. This means no strike is wasted. What may have appeared to be a failure is actually setting you up for victory. Persistence produces winners, and winners tend to carry that persistent attitude throughout life. James 1:12 (NIV) says, "Blessed is the man who perseveres under trial, for when he has stood the test he will receive the crown of life, which God has promised to those who love Him."

Perseverance is the qualification for your crowning. Those who quit when the going gets tough never receive the crown of life. Your character is built in the face of challenges; therefore, your attitude toward challenges will determine the quality of your character. Anytime you are going through a tough day or season of life, don't give up–your character is being tested. When you persevere through trials, you are passing a test that will eventually qualify you for a crown.

When I was going through my divorce, I was subjected to very harsh terms and conditions. I suffered pain beyond words and even considered giving up the custody of my children to my ex-husband. When that thought came to mind, I imagined the pain my decision would result in—and I knew I couldn't inflict myself with perpetual pain for temporary pleasure.

In the face of the seemingly endless court proceedings, I chose to persevere. I held on, even when it made no sense. My character was tested in ways I can't even explain. When Job was tried and tested on every side, his wife asked him in rage, "Are you still maintaining your integrity? Curse God and die!" (Job 2:9 NIV).

When you choose to maintain your integrity in the face of intense trials, be assured that some of your closest allies will advise you to throw in the towel. Resist the temptation to do so. Understand that challenges are there to test the quality of your character. If you maintain your integrity and refuse to compromise, you will receive the crown of life.

Pain is a feeling no one wants, but it's impossible to go through life and not experience some form of suffering. Since pain is inevitable, we must learn how to use it to our advantage. Pain comes through failure, loss, tragedy, unpleasant experiences, wrong choices—and it often results in inactivity. Inactivity is a state where a person gives up hope and stops pursuing anything in life. This attitude toward life leads to regret later in life. And the pain of regret is indescribable.

Regret is worse than the pain of failure and discipline put together. Even in failure, an attempt was made. You can't fail if you didn't try. Regret is much more painful because it results from failing to even try. Sadly, many people live their lives regretting their inaction. **Action will always trump talking, wishing, complaining, and bickering.** Life responds to action.

When a man sows a seed and waters it, nature responds to him by yielding a harvest. Sowing and watering are actions that must yield fruit. In the same vein, if you act on your dreams every day, life will have no option but to yield to you the result which you desire. On the flip side, if you are simply going through the motions without a specific action plan, regret will be the only result.

It's important not to mistake motion for action. Motion is going through life without an action plan, whereas action is working toward a specific goal in mind. Don't just go through the motions. You need a compelling reason to take action every day. When I first decided to write this book, I would think about the idea over and over without taking any action toward it. Months went by, and one morning I woke up feeling very unhappy because I knew I had an idea that I wasn't doing anything about. Your dream will never come to fruition until you start doing something about it.

The feelings of regret often come from the things we know we should do but fail to do. When you fail to act on the ingenuity of your mind, you are bound to experience war on the inside. The greatest war we can ever experience is the one that goes on within us. This was the war I was battling in my mind during the months I failed to do anything about the book I had envisioned. I was so busy fantasizing about the things I would do after the book was completed that I failed to get started.

It only takes one day to get started on an idea, but it takes months and sometimes years to develop the idea into a finished project. This process requires daily, deliberate action. This is where discipline becomes a must-have. Having discipline may look like punishment and deprivation at times, but if you stick with it, you will begin to achieve success.

Think about the pain you will experience in the future if you fail to act today. By linking pain to your inaction, you are giving yourself the power to do whatever it takes to avoid regret in the future. Remember nothing will happen unless you try. Nothing will change until you change your pattern. Don't let days, months, and years pass you by. Act now and avoid the pain of regret in the future. It's never too late to act.

You are responsible for the accomplishment of the dreams you hold within you. When you start taking action, never give less than your best. The last thing you want to do is get to the end of the day wishing you had done better. Avoid that feeling by giving your all every day. Whatever your hands find to do—do it well. Refuse to be among those who get to the finish line only to wish they had put in more effort. If you have more to give, then give more. If you can do more, then do more. Don't let anyone tell you what you can or cannot do.

You are in charge of your life. Develop a work ethic that will place you in a category all by yourself. When you fail to demand more of yourself, you resort to competing with others—and no one ever wins by competing with others. Just be the best you can be, and no one will be able to compete with you.

The story of Cain and Abel is very fitting here. Cain was very angry because God favored Abel's sacrifice over his sacrifice. In Genesis 4:6-7 (NIV), the Lord said to Cain, "Why are you angry? Why is your face downcast? If you do what is right, will you not be accepted? But if you do not do what is right, sin is crouching at your door; it desires to have you, but you must rule over it." In other words, we don't have to compare what we have to what others have.

If you want to possess all that God has in store for you then you must be willing to give your very best. Some people act like Cain when they fail to fully apply themselves but still expect a great reward. They become jealous and angry when others are rewarded for giving their all. The best way to avoid being caught up in a competitive cycle is to give your all, in all you do. When you do the very best you can, you will have no rivalry. You will be filled with contentment, knowing you did the best you could.

TAKE DOMINION

9
PREPARED FOR OPPORTUNITY

Preparation will turn an ordinary person into a genius in the face of opportunity. The impossible can happen when preparation collides with the right moment. Preparation is the time you spend honing your skills, and it is often done in private.

We look at certain people and wonder at their ingenuity, but we fail to acknowledge that people are rewarded in public for what they have practiced over the years in private. You cannot be in the spotlight if you have not been practicing behind closed doors. The future belongs to those who prepare for it. Some people are passively waiting for an opportunity without doing anything in the meantime. Opportunity graces those who are preparing for one.

Each day you wake up, you are blessed with the opportunity to prepare for your dreams. Your preparation will attract the opportunity. Sometimes, we find ourselves pursuing the opportunity but in reality, opportunity responds to preparation. Whatever you want to become you must prepare to become. You must train your mind to see who you want to become. You've got to see the invisible. Only those who can see the invisible can achieve the impossible. This is the hardest part of preparing yourself for what you want. You ought to have a mental picture of who you want to become. You need to be able to describe the idea you have to those who can help you.

This is where a lot of people will get discouraged because you are trying to get others to see something that is not yet there. In this stage, you must be prepared to receive rejection from people. Not everyone will be able to see the unseen. Some people will even try to discredit your idea, but you cannot base the authenticity of your dreams on the opinion of someone who lacks faith in you. You've got to be prepared to defend your idea at all costs. You've got to be bold and unapologetic about what you want out of life. It is your right to be you and no one has the right to tell you what you cannot become. Those who only seek validation from others will accomplish very little.

There will be a select few who will buy into your ideas, but you will never find them until you actually start to work on your ideas. These people will train, encourage, and support you along the way. When you are completely sold on your idea it will show in your behavior. You will find yourself taking bold steps toward your dreams. But it all begins with you. No one is going to hand you something you are not prepared for. You've got to demand more of yourself than anyone else would ever expect from you. Don't confine yourself to the four walls of the familiar places you are comfortable with. Dare to step out into the unfamiliar space where your ideas will be actualized.

It is hard to prepare for the future when you are experiencing turbulence in the present. But in spite of whatever is going on in your life right now, you can decide to prepare for better days. Don't get so consumed with today's storm that you fail to prepare for tomorrow's sunshine.

Years ago, when I was in a turbulent marriage, it was hard for me to see beyond my pain. There were days when I did nothing but lament about everything that was going wrong in my life. But my self-pity didn't get me anywhere. As long as you pitch your tent in the valley, you will never get to the mountaintop. Nothing changed for me until I began to prepare for an opportunity to live better.

Through my experience, I realized my pain was preparing me to become a warrior. Just like David in the Bible, I was relegated to the background where I was left alone to encounter my true self. Don't despise the time you have to be alone with yourself. Had David not been relegated to tending the sheep, he wouldn't have learned how to fight off bears and lions. Who would have thought that the field where the sheep grazed would be David's training ground? When you are despised and pushed to the side, don't put up a fight. Instead, begin to prepare for what's ahead.

Growing up, I often heard the phrase, "Opportunity comes but once." But how erroneous is that ideology? Opportunities will continuously come and go, but only those who are prepared will grab hold of them. For forty straight days, Goliath appeared morning and evening before the Israelites, yet no one approached him. Goliath did not just show up one time, he showed up consistently for forty days. Opportunities are not one-time events—they happen every day all around us. Everyone was presented with the opportunity to fight Goliath, but only the young man who was prepared went for the kill.

I have found that when we are not prepared for an

opportunity, we tend to make excuses for why we cannot pursue it. David didn't think twice about fighting Goliath because he was prepared. You will not have the time to think through your options in the face of an opportunity—you either go for it, or you don't.

People who are prepared are spontaneous. They trust what they have prepared in private, so they are not bound by fear in public. They approach opportunities with certainty. The Bible records that David ran toward Goliath. "As the Philistine moved closer to attack him, David ran quickly towards the battle line to meet him" (1 Samuel 17:48 NIV).

The way you react to an opportunity shows whether or not you are prepared. Don't let opportunity meet you unprepared. Begin to gradually develop the tools you need for where you are going. Make a commitment to reinventing yourself while you look forward to the opportunity. It doesn't matter what your present situation may look like—prepare anyway. David didn't despise the time he spent in the fields caring for his sheep. Rather, he carried out his assignment without complaining. And right there on the field, he prepared himself for opportunities he wasn't even aware of.

Your experiences are preparing you for the opportunities that lie ahead. If David was not first a shepherd, he wouldn't have become a king. If I hadn't been divorced, I wouldn't have a burning desire to serve those in need. So, don't feel bad about where you've been. The things you have been through, both good and bad, are preparing you for who you are about to become.

God has too much invested in you to give up on you. It

doesn't matter how badly you think you have messed up, God will go to any length to rescue you because He loves you so much. You are God's most prized possession. When God made you, He placed inside of you the capacity to carry everything you would need to go through this life—you simply have to accept it. Therefore, God will not let you go astray. He will never stop drawing you back to Himself.

God has given you a purpose that is proportionate to the deposit He placed inside of you. You have what it takes to accomplish that big dream you hold in your mind. The reason your dream looks gigantic is because you have something even greater inside of you to discover. Sometimes we resist the plan of God for our lives and pursue our own plans instead. But when it is all said and done, we will find ourselves doing exactly what God planned for us from the very beginning.

When God instructed Jonah to go to Nineveh, Jonah thought he knew better than God, so he went in the opposite direction instead. Jonah boarded a ship to escape from God's plan, but God pursued him.

"The Lord sent a great wind on the sea, and such a violent storm arose that the ship threatened to break up" (Jonah 1:4 NIV).

God will interrupt your life when you are going off course because He has so much invested in you. Not all problems are from the devil, as we have been taught to believe. Sometimes God will send a storm, just like He did in the case of Jonah, to call us to order. He will even have a whale swallow us whole, if necessary. After Jonah spent three days in the belly of the whale, God spoke to him again regarding going to Nineveh—

and this time, he obeyed. Jonah was changed by his encounter with God.

God doesn't punish us for no reason. His punishment brings out the treasure in us. Saul of Tarsus was another biblical character God had to bring to order. In Acts Chapter 8 we read that Saul was a murderer and persecutor of Christian believers; but one day, the Lord encountered him on his way to Damascus.

The story continues in Acts 9:3-5 (NIV) saying: "As he neared Damascus on his journey, suddenly a light from heaven flashed around him. He fell to the ground and heard a voice say to him, 'Saul, Saul, why do you persecute me?'

'Who are you, Lord?' Saul asked.

'I am Jesus, whom you are persecuting,' he replied."

After the encounter, Saul was blinded without sight for three days. God asked a Christ follower named Ananias to baptize him, but Ananias was hesitant to baptize Saul saying, "Lord, I have heard from many about this man, how much harm he has done to Your saints in Jerusalem. And here he has authority from the chief priests to bind all who call on Your name." But the Lord said to him, "Go, for he is a chosen vessel of Mine to bear My name before Gentiles, kings, and the children of Israel. For I will show him how many things he must suffer for My name's sake" (Acts 9:13-16 NKJV).

God will stop you in your tracks if He has to. There is a plan and a purpose for your life and God will stop at nothing until you align yourself with your purpose. If you have to be blinded for three days like Saul in order to answer the call of God on your life, then so be it. If you have to be rejected before you are accepted like David, then so be it. You cannot have a Saul-like or David-like testimony without a Saul-like or David-like experience.

Nowadays, people are quick to want what others have without the burden that comes along with it. Wishing to have what others have not only makes you covet, but it could also cause you to lose perspective on your own purpose. There is a difference between wishing you had something and aspiring to achieve something. The former is often born out of lack of contentment, competition, resentment, jealousy, and strife; while the latter is born out of a genuine desire to get more out of life.

Let the lives of others inspire you to reach for higher heights. I have realized that inspiration without action is impotent. Don't wish to have what others have; rather, strive to develop the unparalleled work ethic, discipline, and tenacity that they have. Power does not lie in what a person has. Power comes from what a person chooses to do with what they have. What you have is directly related to what you do. If you do what it takes, you will possess all that hard work provides. This attitude stems from a healthy desire to obtain all that God has for you. I have found that you will never go wrong when you desire what God wants for you. God made you and He knows exactly what is good for you. We cannot afford to waste valuable time opposing the will of God over our lives.

"Woe to those who quarrel with their Maker, those who are nothing but potsherds among the potsherds on the ground. Does the clay say to the potter, "What are you making?" Does your work say, "The potter has no hands"?

Woe to the one who says to a father, "What have you begotten?" Or to a mother, "What have you brought to birth?" (Isaiah 45:9-10 NIV).

It's counterproductive to resist God's plan and purpose for our lives. We will never win doing that. Trusting God's plan is the best way to live, but it doesn't mean we won't encounter any detours, roadblocks, or delays along the way. However, when we do, God has a way of putting us back on track.

Coming to America seemed like I was merging onto the highway of success on the journey of my lifelong dreams. It appeared to be a road that would lead to all I had ever wanted in life. I never thought I would encounter any detours, roadblocks, or delays along the way. I had no idea that I was going to be hated and abandoned by those I loved. I never knew I would end up homeless and broke on the side of the road. I never imagined I was going to experience unimaginable pain. All the things I couldn't foresee were the detours I never expected on the highway I was traveling on.

Although I made mistakes that should have destroyed me, God still preserved me. No one can take you out when God has you in the palm of His hand. The enemy did all he could to destroy me, but God spared my life. God used all the acts of wickedness against me for my elevation.

I am a blessed woman.

I am grateful for the narrow path God led me down. The detours I encountered along the way caused delays on my journey, but delay is never denial.

No one can deny you of your place in life. No one can curse you when God has already blessed you.

No detour can prevent you from reaching your destination because God is masterful at rerouting your journey.

God can make a way where there seems to be no way.

You may be at a dead end right now, wondering how you are going to get back on track. I prophesy to you: God will make a way for you. Just like He divided the Red Sea for the Israelites and made them walk on dry land, He will divide every Red Sea in your life and prepare a road for you to walk on.

THE POWER OF WORDS

Whoever speaks into your ears has access into your heart. When words get into your heart, they gradually begin to form your thoughts, and consequently, they will determine the choices you make.

The words you hear can affect the quality of your life. Eve decided to eat the fruit from the tree of the knowledge of good and evil after she received counsel from the devil. Adam also ate of the fruit after he received counsel from Eve. The lives of Adam and Eve were changed forever because they acted on the words the devil spoke into their hearts. Before you can make any decision, you must first conceive it in your heart.

Most of the words that enter into our hearts get in through the words we hear. No wonder Proverbs 4:23 (NIV) says, "Above all else, guard your heart, for everything you do flows from it." The heart will meditate on what enters into it through the ears. The words we hear are very powerful—they can either bless us or curse us. The best place to seek wise counsel is from the Word of God. If you must seek counsel outside of God's Word, then it must come from a person who receives direction from God. Blessed people seek counsel from the Word of God and from godly people.

My first marriage was rocky from the start because I neither sought counsel from the Lord nor did I seek counsel from a godly source. I didn't go through marriage counseling because I didn't know the importance of it. However, ignorance is no excuse because I suffered the consequences of failing to do what was necessary. Seeking wise counsel would have saved me a lot of pain because I would have chosen a godly man for a husband. I suffered the pain of a divorce and everything that came with it because I didn't have a godly counselor in my life.

A godly counselor is equipped to direct a person in making decisions that will bless their lives. We live in a world where everyone seems to have an opinion about everything. **Anyone can have an opinion but not everyone can provide counsel.** Not everyone is equipped to counsel you. Any counsel that is not in line with the truth of God's word is not worth receiving.

A wise person will only receive godly counsel. They won't even listen to other voices. Proverbs 1:5 (NKJV) says, "A wise man will hear and increase learning, and a man of understanding will attain wise counsel." Wise people seek to learn more, and godly counsel increases their learning. Foolish people do the exact opposite. Foolish people don't seek to learn, they only rely on their own feelings or the opinions of their friends about the issues in their lives.

Seeking godly counsel doesn't suggest weakness on the

part of the seeker, it reveals strength because only the wise can admit they need counsel. When you are equipped with sound knowledge from personal study and godly counsel, it will show in the quality of the decisions you make. Our decisions determine our future, so we've got to take them seriously.

An interesting story that comes to mind is that of Rehoboam, son of Solomon in 1 Kings 12:3-18. Rehoboam's first assignment as king was to address the working conditions of his servants. His servants pleaded with him to lighten the burden his father, Solomon, had put on them. He instructed them to return after three days for an answer. While his servants were gone, he consulted with elders who advised him to be kind to his servants. Rehoboam disregarded the advice of the elders and consulted the young men he grew up with instead. The young men advised him to make the working conditions of his servants worse than they were in the past. Rehoboam's decision to punish his servants even more led to the people turning away from him completely.

Godly counsel can help us make better decisions, but it's useless if we don't receive it. Rehoboam received godly counsel from the elders, but he disregarded it. The difference between wisdom and foolishness is the application of knowledge. Wise people receive counsel and apply it to their lives, while foolish people disregard it. When we disregard wise counsel, we are likely to keep searching until we find the advice that aligns with what we want to hear. This is often destructive, as we see in the case of Rehoboam.

When we fail to take the good, we are left with the bad. Remember any counsel that doesn't align with the Word of

God should be discarded, irrespective of who is giving it. Ungodly counsel could come from anywhere—even from the people you love the most—so don't let your emotions blind your judgment.

DELAY IS NOT DENIAL

"Delay is not denial" is my mother's favorite saying and it has become a constant reminder for me as I journey through life. Whenever I get frustrated with delays in any area of my life, my mother always reminds me that delay isn't denial. I have grown to appreciate this truth because I have never experienced any form of delay that denied me of my blessings.

Habakkuk 2:3 (NKJV) says, "For the vision is yet for an appointed time; but at the end it will speak, and it will not lie. Though it tarries, wait for it; because it will surely come, it will not tarry." There is a set time for your miracle. Just like a time-release capsule, your miracle is designed to be released at a set time in your life. A delay cannot deny you of your place in destiny.

Delays only strengthen your faith and reveal the power of God in you. The woman with the issue of blood battled with her condition for 12 years, but at the set time she received her miracle. The children of Israel were under captivity for 40 years, but at the set time they were liberated. I say to you again, delay is not denial. Don't be tricked into believing that the delay you are experiencing is a denial of your blessings.

A delay could also be a blessing in disguise. When we are delayed, we tend to appreciate the process of birthing a miracle. The process is what builds our faith and character.

We've got to understand that a promise requires a process. The process often looks like delay, but the process is required for the fulfillment of the promise. When God gives you a promise, you've got to be willing to go through the process for the fulfillment of the promise.

Every promise that God has given me, I have received in the course of time. Because God cannot lie and because His promises are sure, I rest assured that the promises I have yet to see will happen at the set time. One of the promises that came to pass for me in 2016 was the return of my mother to the United States. I waited four years for this to happen. In 2012, I was pregnant with my second child and my mother had to return back to Nigeria from the United States to have her visa renewed. I was two months away from my delivery date when she left, and I had no doubt in my mind that she was coming back. At this point in time, I was already separated from my ex-husband, so I was in dire need of my mother's presence. I was heartbroken when my mother was denied a visa to return back to the United States.

The following year, she applied again and was denied a second time. I can't tell you how devastated I was when it became evident that she wasn't returning as soon as I had anticipated. During that time, I cried for many nights, but my mother's absence became a pivotal moment in my life. I had no choice but to become the woman I was created to be. Had my mother returned any sooner than she did, I wouldn't have matured as authentically as I did. The process of waiting on my promise resulted in the building of my character. What seemed to be a disappointment and a delay turned out to be part of the process of fulfilling God's promise for my life.

Through the years of being separated from my mother, she would always remind me that "delay is not denial." And I am saying the same thing to you today. Whatever God has promised you, He will bring to pass. Have no fear—God is able to do what He has promised.

God promises to answer us whenever we call on Him. I recall one of my mother's teachings on how God answers prayers. She said when we pray to God for anything that is in line with His will for our lives, He will do one of three things: First, He could answer us right away by providing our request. Second, He could also say, "Not this, take that," because he knows what is best for us. Thirdly, He could say, "Wait, not now."

The third response is the one we don't handle too well. Most of us get frustrated during the waiting period and if we are not careful, we could begin to doubt the promise. During those four years of waiting for my mother's return, the only thing that kept me from doubting my promise was her favorite mantra: delay is not denial. I held onto that phrase as though my life depended on it. I was so certain that my mother was going to return, so I began to make plans for her arrival. I got a room ready for her a year and a half before she arrived. While I was making all of these plans I had no guarantee that she was coming, but I was certain that the promise of God can never fail.

No institution, no man nor woman, no power nor principality can stop God's promise from coming to pass in your life. If God has promised you anything, consider it done! Don't worry about the ticking of the clock. Just remain faithful and fix your eyes on the promise. Though you may not see it, believe that God is working everything out for your good. At the set time, you will have your promise.

TAKE DOMINION

10
LIFE IS HARD

Make no mistake: life is hard. If life were easy, then everyone would be successful.

Though some have had more challenging experiences than others, we can all agree that life is challenging. The sun shines both on the rich and the poor. Both the fortunate and less fortunate experience rejection, disappointment, discrimination, failure, loss, and insecurities. Life is not a respecter of gender, economic status, family values, background, or education. Life will happen to you, so long as you are living in this place called earth.

God made a perfect world until sin entered the heart of man, and since then life has been hard. Knowing this truth about life is very important so we don't spend valuable time asking questions like, "Why do bad things happen to good people?" The answer is, life happens to everybody, both good and bad. Being prepared for life is the best way to live. Now, I don't mean we should live our lives in anticipation that something bad is going to happen. But it's necessary to prepare ourselves, knowing that no matter what happens, we will overcome.

Faith is necessary to live life with certainty. No wonder the Bible says, "Who shall separate us from the love of Christ? Shall tribulation, or distress, or persecution, or famine, or nakedness, or peril, or sword?... Yet in all these things we are more than conquerors through Him who loved us. For I am persuaded that neither death nor life, nor angels nor principalities nor powers, nor things present nor things to come, nor height nor depth, nor any other created thing, shall be able to separate us from the love of God which is in Christ Jesus our Lord" (Romans 8:35-39 NKJV).

I wouldn't have survived what I went through had I not had faith in Jesus Christ. There were times when my life would have been over, but God spared me. I remember being thrown out on the street twice by my ex-husband in less than a year of being in the United States. On both occasions, I ended up at a homeless shelter. The first time, I had only $20 in my purse when I got to the shelter, but for some reason, I was at peace because I knew God was with me.

Within two days of being at the shelter, I was spotted by a lady who worked there as a counselor. She pulled me to the side and asked me how I got there. After I explained what had happened, she told me that the shelter wasn't safe and that I needed to return home. She took me to her house, contacted my ex-husband's family, and I returned to them.

The second time I ended up at the shelter, I was pregnant with my first child. A woman I met at the shelter this time told me that "any man that physically abuses you is not worthy of you". After a week and a half, I told the shelter workers that I was returning to my ex-husband. They bid me farewell but advised me of the dangers of going back with a warning, "Abusers don't stop being abusive until they receive help."

Sometimes we make life harder than it should be because of the decisions we make. My life was harder than it should have been because I chose to marry a person I shouldn't have married. I was ignorant of the consequences of my actions at the time, but that didn't stop the consequences from coming. Although God has a way of turning our sorrows into joy, we are still responsible for the consequences of our decisions. But this is how we gain wisdom from our own experiences. The consequences of marrying the wrong person shaped my life and today, I am better for it.

Life is hard, but we can live better when we begin to apply the lessons we've learned from our own experiences and from the experiences of those who have walked down the same road. **Too often people want to know what others do to be successful, but the real power lies in what they don't do.**

Psalms 1:1 (NKJV) begins by telling us what a blessed man wouldn't do: "Blessed is the man who walks not in the counsel of the ungodly, nor stands in the path of sinners, nor sits in the seat of the scornful."

This is the recipe for success. If you know what not to do and you don't do it, you will succeed. Because my previous marriage failed, I know exactly what not to do before and after one gets married. If you avoid the don'ts you automatically embrace the do's; but to apply these successfully, you must know the difference. Life is hard, but if you are willing to learn, you will live better.

Think of life as a teacher and you as the student. Life will instruct, correct, and punish us accordingly. It's in our best interest to be good students who learn from life's teachings and advance from one level to the next. Life's teachings are in the form of experiences and they happen all around us. If we pay attention to the events around us, we will learn from them and become better. If we fail to pay attention to life and learn what is necessary for growth, we will continue to repeat the same mistakes over and over.

I often hear people complain that life is unfair. Life may be unfair, but we can't afford to dwell on the unfair things that happen in our lives. The healthy way to live life is to expect good things to happen in your life. Proverbs 23:18 tells us that our expectations will not be cut short. Expectation brightens your day. It gives you a reason to go for what you want, knowing you will get it. And even when you don't get it, you remain expectant knowing that you will have another opportunity to get it. Each new day is a brand-new opportunity for you to go at it again. Life responds to those who have chosen not to give up, no matter what. You and I can become one of those who compel life to give up what it has in store for us because of our approach.

Life's experiences can rip our lives apart so quickly, leaving bits and pieces everywhere that don't make sense. But, in the process of time, the bits and pieces will come together. It could take years, or even decades, to put the pieces of our lives back together—but it is possible.

No experience in your life will be wasted. Everything happens on purpose—nothing happens by accident. None of my experiences made sense to me at the time I was going through them, and I was almost tempted to believe I had no purpose at all. But that was a lie. Just because your purpose is associated with pain doesn't make it useless. The experience that couldn't break you will eventually make you. **Overcoming**

a bad experience is great, but the greater blessing lies in who you are becoming as a result.

You may have had experiences that left you shattered in pieces, but eventually those pieces will come together. I felt my life was in pieces after I encountered several major losses. I didn't understand why I lost my father the year prior to marrying the person he didn't approve of. I didn't understand why I left Nigeria for the United States only to experience the most horrific years of my life. I didn't understand why I had to restart my life in a foreign country without my family. I didn't understand why I had to lose a brother and not have the opportunity to attend his funeral. I didn't understand why I had to deal with an ex-husband who was committed to making my life miserable.

I found myself at the lowest point of my life, in a valley with all kinds of problems around me. I liken my experience to that of Ezekiel who encountered God in a valley full of dry bones. In the valley, God instructed Ezekiel to prophesy to the dry bones and he did. "So I prophesied as I was commanded; and as I prophesied, there was a noise, and suddenly a rattling; and the bones came together, bone to bone. Indeed, as I looked, the sinews and the flesh came upon them, and the skin covered them over; but there was no breath in them. Also He said to me, "Prophesy to the breath, prophesy, son of man, and say to the breath, 'thus says the Lord God: "Come from the four winds, O breath, and breathe on these slain, that they may live." So I prophesied as He commanded me, and breath came into them, and they lived, and stood upon their feet, an exceedingly great army," (Ezekiel 37:7-9 NKJV).

I encountered God like never before when I was in the valley. All the prophesies that were spoken over my life came flooding back to me like a rushing river sweeping through my life, gathering all the pieces together.

There's life in the Word of God. Jesus raised Lazarus from the dead with a spoken word. Every miracle happens with a spoken word. Perhaps, you are in a valley full of dry bones today. If you are, it's time for you to rise up and prophesy the Word of God over your life. The Word of God is God Himself. Everything responds to the Word of God because everything was created by the Word. That is why John 1: 1-3 (NKJV) says, "In the beginning was the Word, and the Word was with God, and the Word was God. He was in the beginning with God. All things were made through Him, and without Him nothing was made that was made."

You can recreate your life by speaking the Word of God. Search for Bible verses that address your situation and pray like you've never prayed before. That is what it takes to put your life back together. Everything else will pass away, but the Word of God will last forever.

There were times when I was so frustrated with my experiences and I often hoped that something magical would happen someday that would change my life forever. Well, that never happened. I have come to realize that life is not mystical. You will never wake up to discover that all of your problems are gone if you don't do anything about them before going to bed. You will always wake up to the reality you have created for yourself the day before.

I came across a quote that reads, "If you woke up broke,

- 176 -

you had no business going to sleep." You cannot afford to be sleeping all night and taking naps during the day when you have problems to solve. Sleep is a luxury, especially if you are far from achieving your goals. Sleep is sweet when you have accomplished something for the day. You cannot wake up to a new life if you have not taken the time to create one.

Problems will typically grow from bad to worse if you do nothing about them. If anything stays at a spot for too long, it begins to decay. Sadly, some people die in their youth and get buried in their old age. Stagnation is dying in slow motion. Life will only respond to you when you put something out there. If you do nothing, then life will punish you because you are occupying space without contribution. Your contribution is your payment for living rent-free on earth. We all enjoy the benefits of living on earth and we are responsible for making this world better than we found it.

Life will yield to you if you are a contributor. There is nothing mystical about that. If we don't work, then we don't deserve to eat. If we fail to pursue the dreams that we hold in our minds, then life will be worthless. If we fail to do what is necessary to live a productive life, then we will become mediocre. In the same vein, if we go after our dreams with all we've got, then we will have all that we want.

I remember having a conversation with a former co-worker who was concerned about receiving a verbal warning due to tardiness. He inquired if I had ever received a verbal warning for tardiness and I said no. He was rather shocked by my response and wondered why I had a "perfect standing" as he called it. He then went on to say that he was going to rub my hand to get some "good luck." To which I said, "You don't have to rub my hand for good luck. What you need to do is wake up as soon as your alarm clock goes off in the morning and you will get to work on time."

Success is that simple! So often, we act like my former co-worker who thinks there is a good luck charm somewhere that produces the magic required for daily productivity. But the magic is in what you train yourself to do. **It's interesting how the hardest working people are often considered to be "the lucky ones" by those who fail to put in the work required to produce results.**

Lazy people would rather depend on luck than work, but what they fail to realize is that luck rewards only those who work. You get lucky when you are actively working on your goals. You cannot depend on luck to succeed, but you can depend on work because it produces guaranteed results. Quit thinking that there is some lucky charm you need to find in order to succeed in life. You cannot shake hands with a successful person and suddenly become successful yourself. However, if you study what they have done and do the same, then you are likely to have a shot at being successful in the same way they are.

Years ago, I met a lady who was preparing for a professional examination and she told me how she was going to meet with a prophet for prayers. Apparently, all her friends who took the examination prior received prayers from the prophet and passed. I thought to myself, seeking prayers from a prophet alone cannot guarantee success in an examination. If you pray and you don't study, you are likely to fail. Don't get miracles confused with magic. Magic will mean not studying the subject matter and expecting to pass. Miracles, on the other hand, are beyond human comprehension. Everyone I know or have read about who has experienced a miracle played a part in the miracle process.

Jesus performed His first miracle of turning water into wine at a wedding after the wedding servants filled the jars with water (John 2:7). Jesus fed five thousand people with five loaves and two fish after his disciples gathered all the food available from a young boy in the crowd (Matthew 14:17-18). The woman with the issue of blood got healed after she touched the hem of Jesus' garment (Luke 8:44).

Now, Jesus could have performed these miracles in spite of the actions of the people involved, but I think He wants us to see a pattern. The pattern is clear: an action is required on your part for you to receive a miracle. No wonder James 2:26 (NKJV) says, "For as the body without the spirit is dead, so faith without works is dead also." Faith alone is not enough because if you really believe in something, you will act on it. Therefore, inaction is an indication of a lack of faith. Faith is potent when action follows. Begin to act on your dreams like you believe they will happen—and they will.

THERE IS TIME FOR EVERYTHING

Time is so precious. We all have 24-hours in a day, yet some people accomplish more than others in the same amount of time. It could be tempting to look at someone else's life and become intimidated by their level of success, forgetting that we are all working with the same amount of the commodity called time.

The way we utilize our time will determine the outcome we get at the end of the day. When we set goals with a timeline, we don't always achieve the results we want, but we always have an outcome. Results are likely, but outcomes are constant. You will always have an outcome at the end of each day so it's important you plan your day before it starts. Never begin your day, week, month, or year without a plan. When you fail to plan, you are making room for anything to happen.

Time will pass whether we make wise use of it or not. Therefore, knowing when to do what is the best thing that can happen to anyone. The book of Ecclesiastes is a great resource for understanding the place of time in our lives by giving us a practical way to spend our time. Chapter 3, verses 1-8, (NKJV) says it this way:

"To everything there is a season,

A time for every purpose under heaven:

A time to be born,

   And a time to die;

A time to plant,

   And a time to pluck what is planted;

 A time to kill,

   And a time to heal;

A time to break down,

   And a time to build up;

 A time to weep,

   And a time to laugh;

A time to mourn,

   And a time to dance;

A time to cast away stones,
    And a time to gather stones;
A time to embrace,
    And a time to refrain from embracing;
A time to gain,
    And a time to lose;
A time to keep,
    And a time to throw away;
 A time to tear,
    And a time to sew;
A time to keep silence,
    And a time to speak;
A time to love,
    And a time to hate;
A time of war,
    And a time of peace."

Life is full of contrasts, but we all have to learn how to function in spite of them. Sometimes we experience losses and at other times we celebrate gains. I have mourned the loss of loved ones and in the same token, I have learned to celebrate life and all the goodness it offers. Don't let life keep you in a state of perpetual mourning because after mourning comes dancing.

Some people are still mourning over something they lost 20 years ago, and that is a very unhealthy way to live. When we refuse to get over a loss, we rob ourselves of the joy and celebration that comes afterward. God is not focused on what you have lost, He will always use what you have left to bless you. Rather than focus on your loss, focus on your gain. The loss of a job, marriage, or opportunity is not worth mourning for the rest of your life. It's okay to mourn your loss for a season, but you've got to know when it's time to wash your face and sing a new song.

Losing a loved one is heart-wrenching and overwhelming. The morning I received the call that my brother had passed, I remember crying, screaming, and shaking in unbelief. For weeks, I was numb and unable to function. Though I knew he had gone to be with the Lord, my heart was broken. Gradually, I began to come to terms with my brother's passing and as difficult as it was, I learned to celebrate life again.

I have come to realize that guilt can keep people in a state of perpetual mourning. Guilt comes from the failure to do what we can, when we can. Don't wait until it is too late to express your love for people. Don't wait until it is too late to forgive—it's not worth holding unto. Let it go. Sometimes we don't realize that we don't have all the time in the world to do the things we can. It's time to start expressing love, kindness, patience, kindness, and tolerance to those in your life. Don't hold back what you know you can give.

THE POWER IN YOUR STORY

What is your story? Your story is your interpretation of the events in your life. After events happen in your life, your interpretation of them becomes your story. Ironically, two people can have similar experiences with two entirely different interpretations. That is the power of interpretation. You can retell an event, after it has happened, in a way that is empowering or disempowering.

After my divorce, I didn't want to share my story because I was so embarrassed by it. The feeling of embarrassment stemmed from the negative interpretation I had given my experience. I felt like a failure, so my interpretation made me feel ashamed of my experience. I battled with this feeling of failure until I realized I had the power to change the narrative I was telling myself. I began to learn how to share my story in a positive way.

Going through a divorce was a painful experience for me, but I have become indestructible because of it. Your story is a combination of experiences that have brought you to where you are now. Your story is personal. Others can tell it in part, but your story cannot be told in totality by anyone but you. It's your personal journey toward your destiny.

As you recount your life's experiences, always look for the good in every experience that looks bad. You may have been through something traumatic but think about the champion you have become. Think about the wisdom you have gained in the area that once overwhelmed you. Think about the clarity of purpose you now have because of the experience that once challenged your very existence. Think about the confidence you now possess because life compelled you to get out of your comfort zone. Begin to see how your experiences can empower, rather than disempower you.

You cannot share a story that will inspire people if you don't feel empowered by it yourself. If your story doesn't empower you, then you need to change your narrative. You are the author of your script and you can rewrite the script to reflect victory and not defeat. Change your perception and tell your story in a positive way that will inspire others. You've got to own your story and tell it in the best way you can.

Be authentic and relatable in your delivery. People will connect with your story when they think you are just like them. There are people all around the world who are waiting to hear your story. Your story has the power to spark up a revolution in the lives of those you've been called to help. You have been given that unique experience for a reason, and you are responsible for sharing it in a way that is inspiring to others.

Your story fuels your purpose. I am currently working on providing a transitional home for women who are separated, divorced, or experiencing domestic violence. When I was undergoing domestic abuse in my previous marriage, I checked into a homeless shelter on two occasions, and my being there showed me what I needed to do for others when I got out. I have always wanted to empower women, but I didn't know how. Being at the homeless shelter showed me a void that I could fill around me.

We were created to be the hands and feet of Jesus. You are the answer to someone else's prayer. You are the solution to the problems around you. God allowed you to go through certain experiences so that you could show others how to deal with similar situations. Your story is a testimony that God is at work in your life. You don't share your story for fame—you share your story to give God glory and liberate others.

God will use every experience you've had for His glory— even the ugliest ones. He will use the experiences that you are too embarrassed to talk about, the ones that have people talking about you, the ones you wish you could re-live, and the ones you wish you could erase from your history. All of your experiences have their purpose, and you will see the connection between your experiences as you begin to change your narrative.

Your life is not an accident. When you come full-circle you will appreciate every event that has happened to you and for you. Don't question your purpose because of one horrible event that happened in your life. First Lady Serita Jakes always says, "Your misery will become your ministry." Is that true of your life? I can say that about mine because if I didn't go through a divorce, I wouldn't be involved in half of the things I am involved in today. **Your pain will always redirect you to your purpose.**

Pastor Lisa Osteen Comes recently shared her story at a conference I attended, and it was very powerful. She grew up in a household of faith. Growing up, she wanted to get married, be in ministry, and have children. She got married right after college and thought she was set for life. Shortly after, her husband deceived her by sending her back to her parents only to send her divorce papers in the mail. She was heartbroken and devastated by that experience. Lisa's father was a pastor and he suggested they tell the church about her divorce so they could pray for her. Lisa was very hesitant at first, but she eventually agreed to share her divorce story with the congregation. After the service that day, some men and women who were going through similar situations approached Lisa for prayer. Lisa was amazed at the response she received from those in the crowd. What looked like the worst period of her life became the most influential. Lisa began to minister to people who were hurting just like her, and her pain became her ministry. Today, Lisa is remarried with children, and she is living the life she was born to live.

I am also a witness that no experience is wasted. Everything I have been through has only qualified me for where I am today.

You have dominion over every experience in your life. You are in your domain. You rule over every situation in your life. You are a territorial commander. Whatever you decree with your mouth and believe in your heart, you shall have in your life. I loose you from every shackle that has held your down all this time. I annul every lie the enemy has spoken against you about your experience, in the name of Jesus—I declare it null and void.

You are liberated!

You are loosed!

Take back your power and take back your authority. Dominion is yours for the taking. Take your rightful place here on earth. Assume your position. Take hold of what has already been given to you. Moving forward, you will rule over your adversaries. You will decree, and it shall come to pass. You are armed and dangerous. You are hereby anointed to dominate!

Sit on your throne. Take Dominion.

ACKNOWLEDGMENTS

I am who I am today by the grace of God. I have come thus far because of the love and support of my family.

To my father, I thank you for giving me the audacity to be myself. Because of the way you raised me, I've never felt intimidated by greatness. You made me believe that greatness is attainable.

To my beloved mother, I thank you for supporting me in all I do. You nurtured me into the woman I am today. I wouldn't be doing what I'm doing if you weren't here with me. For that reason, and many more, I honor you.

To my brothers, you protect me like a lion and instruct me like a teacher. I thank you for allowing me to shine, always.

To my sister, thank you for seeing in me what I couldn't see in myself. Your prophecies have manifested in my life. You love me just the way I am, and I thank you.

To my husband, the king over my house, I thank you for loving me unconditionally. From the day I met you, I knew you were my husband. I'm honored to be your wife. Thank you for protecting my heart.

To my precious children, I love you beyond words. You are the reason I do what I do.

To my beloved Aunt, Mrs. Ethel Spiff, you are full of love and wisdom. Thank you for covering and protecting me like your own. To the woman of God in my life, Mrs. Mojibola Igbinyemi, thank you for loving me through and through. You are the most consistent person I've ever met.

To my friend, Mrs. Judy Vaughan, thank you for your unconditional love and relentless prayers. You wrote the most authentic and God-inspired foreword I've ever read.

To my editor, Amy Noelck, thank you for being part of this project. Your beautiful spirit inspires me to write even more. Thank you for the brilliant ideas you gave me during this journey.

To my photographer and designer, Enoch Odu, thank you to you and your entire team. You literally brought my dreams to life.

To my beautiful friends, Monica, Danielle, and Karen, thank you for being so genuine. You ladies show me so much love and I thank you.

To all the people who have read and are being inspired by this book, I am honored to be part of your journey. You will always have a special place in my heart.

www.ingramcontent.com/pod-product-compliance
Lightning Source LLC
LaVergne TN
LVHW051052080426
835508LV00019B/1835